Jean Philippe Lecat

THE GOLDEN BOOK OF
BURGUNDY

BONECHI

CONTENTS

Printed in Italy by Centro Stampa Editoriale Bonechi.

Translated by Helen Seale, Traduco, s.n.c., Florence

Diffusion: OVET PARIS - 13, Rue des Nanettes - Paris 11 - Tél.43 38 56 80

CREDITS

Photos from the archives of CASA EDITRICE BONECHI *taken by* Paolo Giambone.
G. Dagli Orti *pages 12, 42-47, 51a, 56, 57, 59b, 60, 62a, 71b.*
Pinheira *page19.*
The other photographs were supplied by "La Goélette" *pages 70a, 102a,c.*
J.P.Muzard, Beaune *page77*
Hôtel de Ville of Saulieu, *page 117d.*
The photos on pages 66, 76, 107, 116b, are uncredited.

ISBN 88-7009-222-4

* * *

A «JOYFUL ENTRANCE»

When a community of Burgundy prepared to receive its Duke for the first time, there was the most extraordinary flurry of activity for weeks beforehand. Doors and walls were decorated with banners and foliage, platforms were set up for the «tableaux vivants» depicting the Prophets of the Old Testament and nude «mermaid-like» girls, and processions of confraternities and guilds were organized. In large towns, painters, sculptors and musicians were mobilized. The mansions of the nobility were covered with flowered tapestries. The fountains at the cross-roads dispensed rose water and Beaune wine. The civilian troops paraded noisily... In the lava-roofed villages the celebrations were much humbler. But what a lot of enthusiasm went into preparing the festivities! People sang as they brought junipers down from the mountain to plant along the roadside leading to the church and they sang as they covered the barns with cloths decorated with wild flowers; the curate repeatedly told the boys dressed in tatters that they would accompany him to the altar.

On the morning of the great day, the authorities went down into the street to meet the sovereign. At Dijon the city representatives, dressed in violet-coloured velvet, looked like princes; in this most remote village they certainly behaved as such. The Duke placed his foot on the ground and greeted them kindly. He was usually very thirsty and was pleased to accept a glass of local wine: Chambertin, Romanée, Musigny, Montrachet... or even some of that sour white wine, the medieval recipe for which has, fortunately, been lost. The Duke praised the wine and chatted in a familiar way on the edge of the road. Then the prince and his escort got back onto their horses. A band preceded them with a fanfare of fifes and drums in the cities, and hurdy-gurdies and fiddles in the countryside. The Duke rode along the main street with the mayor at his right side. The children watched, their eyes open wide; the ladies dreamed, under the sullen gaze of their husbands, as they watched the blonde curls of the angel-faced pages; the crowds sang the old Christian shout of joy: «Noel, Noel!». The power was strong and beautiful. The people of Burgundy recognized it from the signs that cannot deceive the wisdom of peasants: and for a long time they carried on talking about «the beautiful grey horse of Monseigneur...»

It was, in those good times, a «Joyful Entrance».

Come with us into an ancient land of the West which owes nearly all of its visible shape to the patient and inspired work of Man. History is in command here. In order to understand it, it is necessary to pay attention. Just like the Dukes of long ago, we have to learn how to «place a foot on the ground», taste the fruits of the vine, appreciate the work of the vine-dressers, and take time over the encounter and the festivities.

A Joyful Entrance! Joyeuse Entrée!

Today Burgundy is made up of four French departments – 31.582 Km², 1.600.000 inhabitants – converging on the ancient granite socle of Morvan, covered in mysterious forests, whose springwaters flow, through the Seine, the Loire, the Saône and the Rhône into three seas. The heart consists of a beech-wood giving refuge to herds of wild boar, near the springs which were once considered sacred. All around, the more recent geological ages have created plateaux and valleys, places of transit and of exchange. Geography has set no natural limits and allows for encounter, welcoming, enlightenment, and dispersion...

In this way, for thousands of years, Burgundy has lived through the shock of forgotten cultures: reindeer horns with a silica handle against a leather shield, a stone axe against a bronze helmet, an ash lance against an iron sword. Rome and its art, weapons and laws built free cities on the ruins of Gaul, a shining civilization which dreamt of the one God that the Syrian merchants had revealed. Burgundy owes its name to the Scandinavian people of Burgondes who ended their wandering here in the Vth century. These good giants were taken by what they considered to be the essentialities: bees, vines and pastureland, and they mixed with the Celtic peasants. But at night they used to sing the epic poem of their struggle against Attila: the «Niebelungen». The Christian Middle Ages was one long battle. Thousands of abbeys and priorates led the fighting – at the rhythm of the eight daily offices – from Ireland to Poland, from Sweden to Sicily – against Evil and its iron hand which held the poor in its grip: violence, injustice and wealth. In Burgundy, the inspiration came from Cluny and Citeaux. This was the homeland of all the black monks and white monks of the whole of Europe. The Cluniac Urban II and the Cistercian Bernard, launched the prodigious throngs of Crusaders onto the roads leading to the East.

Burgundy's ambition to create a State was realized between the XIVth and XVth centuries, the flamboyant epos of the «Great Dukes of the West». Under the initial emblem of the «Golden Fleece», the dominions which today make up the Kingdom of the Netherlands and Belgium, the Great Duchy of Luxemburg, and north and eastern France, joined together to create, between the Kingdom of France and the Germanic Empire, a tolerant, prosperous and pacific middle European area, where people had the right to think, pray and love in ten languages. The capital city was Brussels. Dijon continued to be the birthplace and was also the tomb of the founding dynasty within the sumptuous framework of the Carthusian monastery of Champmol, where all the Italian and Flemmish artists met. Charles V was the last of the dream's princes, broken by the national States' desire for power.

The old duchy of Burgundy became French. It was not easy to get used to the new provincial state, subject to governors, superintendents and prefects... The last independent power – the high magistrature – constructed an admirable urban view during the classical period. Then, along the rivers, many Burgundians left the town of their childhood. Others dedicated themselves more than ever to their stony hills, and created marvels. Today Burgundy wine is more famous than Burgundy itself.

But perhaps the story is not over yet.

Spire of the Gate of Burgundy.

SENS

It is not a bad idea to approach Burgundy through the discovery of its rich cereal-growing plains and the active industrial suburbs of the areas bordering Ile-de-France and Champagne, which the modern economy includes as part of the influential area of the Parisian agglomerate. But the history of Sens is really striking.

Sens was the birthplace of a terrible people: the *Sénons*. They seized Rome in the IVth century before our era. While the senators discussed the weight of the gold requested for the ransom, the «war king», *Brennus*, threw his sword onto the scales, shouting: «*Vae Victis, ill luck to the defeated...*». Gangs of Sénons sacked *Delphi* and reached the heart of Asia Minor where they founded an independent Celtic kingdom about which *Saint Paul*, in his *Epistle to the Galatians*, was able to mention their adoration of one God.

Agendicum, the capital of Sénon country – from which the modern name of *Sens* derives – was at the head of Christian Gaul. For fifteen centuries, the archbishop of Sens had pre-eminence over the archbishop of Paris. This explains the presence of the large religious buildings which characterize the city and which saw Popes, Kings, the Council of 1140, during which *Saint Bernard* cen-

sured *Abelard*, and the exile of *Thomas Becket*.

The **Cathedral of Saint-Etienne** is one of the major works of French art – *opus francigenum* – built in the «gothic» style which was to reign all over Europe. It was started in 1140 by the architect Guillaume de Sens, right at the dawning of this new style. The vastness of the project is striking and it was later copied, for example, at Canterbury. Work on the cathedral was recommenced many times. The *Stone Tower*, which is 78 metres high, was rebuilt between the XIVth and the XVth centuries; the two lateral portals are a splendid example of the flamboyant Gothic style; some chapels were added in the XVIIIth century: one of them hosts the *tomb of the Dauphin*, the son of Louis XV, created by Coustou; the choir gate and the canopy on the altar are a final gesture of baroque style. Six centuries of faith...

However large a monument, it is necessary to retain an image of it. Discover the *light of Sens*. In no other place in Burgundy is the dialogue between stone and glass so intense. The elevation of the nave offers an exceptional volume; between the XIIIth and XVIIth centuries, huge stained glass windows were added to touch the souls of the people faced with the vision of the Patriarchs, the

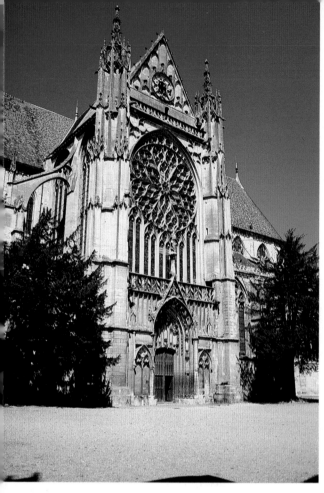

The Cathedral of Saint-Etienne: south transept, western façade and internal view of the nave.

Prophets and the Martyrs. When the deacon Etienne was stoned, evening fell on Jerusalem. Saul of Tarsus looked after the executioners' cloaks. On the road to Damascus he saw a light which, once he became the apostle Paul, he wanted to teach the whole world about. Without doubt the closest we can get to that light is the blend of blue and gold found in the red-coloured sunset of Saint-Etienne in Sens.

The **Synodal Palace** – the seat of the ecclesiastical tribunal – and the **old Archbishopric**, together with the cathedral, make up a group of monuments hosting one of the most beautiful museums of religious art in Burgundy. There are many allusions to the «origins»: signs from the «mists of time» before history began, testimony of Roman Gaul. But in the underground rooms and underneath the high rib vaults, Christian art can be found – from Byzantium to the Nile Valley, from Flanders to the ateliers of Parisian goldsmiths – dazzling us with its variety and coherence: a hundred forms, one Truth... These masterpieces were not created for shop-windows but to serve God. Here respect prevails over curiosity. The Eternal One said to Moses: «*Remove your sandals from your feet, because you are on holy land*».

The Abbey of Saint-Germain.

(Above right) the cathedral of Saint-Etienne; (below) panorama of the city.

AUXERRE

A happy and beautiful town! *Ausserre* – get used to the pronunciation: in Burgundy the X, so vulgar, does not exist – was an important spiritual centre, a big market place for timber and wine, a town of songs and poetry. Today it is an active industrial and agricultural centre. The young parishioners of *Abbot Deschamps* are now a famous football team: one of France's most inventive teams on inspired evenings... It is not surprising that the Irish have always felt so at home here!

Saint-Germain l'Auxerrois – the bishop who gave his name to the parish church of the Kings of France, situated opposite the Louvre – trained Saint Patrick. He shaped the faith of the Apostle of Ireland. It was probably he who revealed the symbol of the *Shamrock* to Saint Patrick – the three-leaved clover – which he needed in the «Verte Erin» to help the Celtic kings of Donegal understand the mystery of the Trinity...

First of all you should go down towards the river, and take in the whole sight from the right bank, revealing the fine view. There are three great religious buildings: the *Cathedral of Saint-Etienne*, the *Abbey of Saint-Germain*

and the *vinedressers' church of Saint Peter* dominate the Yonne which directs the whole region towards the Seine and Paris. The Yonne made Auxerre's fortune. For two thousand years, rivers were the only economically viable means of transport in Europe. A good navigable river which flowed towards interesting markets was the secret of wealth. Long rafts of floating wood came down from Morvan, boats loaded with cereals flowed downstream, and all of this was surrounded by huge vineyards covering the plateaux. A multitude of vine-growers and mariners worked to quench the thirst of medieval Paris where «Burgundy wine» was the wine of Auxerre. The exporting of wine was so profitable that in the XIVth century there were civil riots: the vine-dressers paid by the big landowners were demanding... «forty hours» in order to have some time to cultivate their own vines.

Now go up towards the town. Take the time to walk around and discover it. The town centre is superb, especially around the **Hôtel de Ville (Town Hall)** and the XVth century **Clock Tower**. Here you can meet the «Auxerrois». Their love of wine and taste for big style

trading have given rise to a subtle, shrewd and pleasant spirit. Auxerre has created some beautiful songs and one of them is Burgundy's most moving and serious song.

All French children sing the funny story of «*Cadet Roussel*»:

«*Cadet Roussel a trois maisons
Qui n'ont ni poutres, ni chevrons:
C'est pour loger les hirondelles...*»

The hero of this little story was the bailiff of Auxerre towards the end of the «Ancien Régime». The song ridicules his peculiarities. When the Revolution cast its youth onto the battlefields of Europe, the volunteers from Yonne wanted to take some of the spirit of their homeland with them. An officer composed these lines for them, based on an old tune which went back to the times of the Dukes, creating an ironic and nostalgic march. And so that extravagant character accompanied them from the Pyramids to Moscow... They marched behind a lieutenant-colonel of the same descent as them: *Davout*, who became a field-marshal at 34 years of age, Duke of Auerstaedt and Prince of Eckmühl.

The statue of an old lady will surprise you. This familiar image recalls one of the most important French poetesses of the XXth century: *Marie Noël*. Marie Rouget

The Cathedral of Saint-Etienne, the western façade and the main portal in flamboyant Gothic style.

was as «Auxerroise» as you can be. In solitude, she lived a very touching internal adventure, which inspired the magic form of her popular songs:

> «*Quand il est entré dans mon logis clos,*
> *j'ourlais un drap lourd près de la fenêtre*
> *l'hiver dans les doigts, l'ombre dans le dos...*
> *Sais-je depuis quand j'étais là sans être*
> *Et je cousais, je cousais, je cousais...*
> *Mon coeur, qu'est-ce que tu faisais?*»

Ask for the works of Marie Noël or, for example, André Blanchet's beautiful essay (published by Seghers, 1962). You will know practically all there is to know about Burgundy if you take this lament with you:

> «*On est venu dire à la Reine*
> *Qui dans sa chambre attend le sort,*
> *On est venu dire à la Reine*
> *Le Coeur de votre amour est mort...*»

The Roman frescoes in the crypts, especially those of **Saint-Etienne** and **Saint-Germain** – showing a Christ of light surrounded by bleeding horsemen, immobile suns in the red ochre vaults – will give you a further clue: this country, which seems so familiar to us, has never stopped dreaming about Eternity.

(Right) The Clock Tower; (below left) the statue of Marie-Noël by François Brochet; (right) the three houses of Cadet Roussel.

PONTIGNY

The tenacity of Burgundy. The Abbey of Pontigny was founded in the XIIth century by the «*Citeaux*» *Order*. This order «swarmed» – using the Burgundian image of a beehive – to thirty-four monasteries all over Europe. The abbey had particularly close connections with England: three archbishops of Canterbury, loyal to the apostolic faith, lived there in painful exile. The chuch, which is severe and distinct, is an admirable element of light in the transition from Romanesque to Gothic style. Here, for six centuries, the white monks greeted the dawning of each day with the following joyful words: «*I can hear the Beloved One. Here He comes, skipping like a fawn on the hills*».

You must listen to the silence here.

It is not known why France's political powers considered the monks of Pontigny at first to be unnecessary and, later, to be dangerous. The monks were driven out: first during the Revolution and then at the beginning of the XXth century. But you cannot stop the Spirit from living within the stones.

The philosopher, Paul Desjardins, created a centre for meditation here in 1906. Thomas Mann and François Mauriac, André Gide and Paul Valéry, André Malraux and Pierre Emmanuel came to meditate at Pontigny. Intelligence is a form of exile. T.S. Eliot met the shadow of Thomas Becket, who sang the praises of Pontigny: and he wrote *Murder in the Cathedral*. Today generous people dedicate themselves to outcasts here: the poor and the handicapped. Pontigny remains a sign of life.

The abbatial church of Pontigny.

Chablis, the Golden Gate.

CHABLIS

At last we come to the wine! No doubt you were starting to wonder about this Burgundy with its famous wines which so far has only offered you expanses of cereal-growing plains, pasture-land and forests. Now the two turrets of the *Golden Gate* lead you to the heart of one of France's top vineyards.

You might feel as though you already know this wine since it has been so widely imitated from California to Australia. As though it were enough to elaborate a slightly dry white wine using special vines in order to create a *Chablis*! Land closely bordered by the banks of the Serein is needed; with «beaunois» plants and selected Chardonnay; great care needs to be taken in the pruning, ripening, harvesting and wine-making, the main mysteries of which ten generations of wine-growers are only barely able to control. Young Chablis is a crystal green colour and still tastes of grapes; when aged it changes to a clear gold colour with the addition of strong harmonies.

The *Confraternity of the «Piliers Chablisiens»* holds its assembly on the fourth Sunday of November. It has the confidence of the strong and will do nothing to contest the discovery of other wines from the Yonne area; dry, rich whites from the Chitry and Saint-Pris area; deep, scented reds from around Irancy and Coulanges-la-Vineuse. The Confraternity knows the rarity of its treasure: an average of ten million bottles per year... Here you will make another discovery: a great white wine from Burgundy should be served cool. This means *at cellar temperature* and not ruined by that loathsome modern invention, the ice bucket.

TONNERRE

The history of Tonnerre could inspire a novel. It has existed, firmly entrenched on its rock, since the times of the «Hairy Gaul». Here a countess of Tripoli and Syria became a nun and an extraordinary secret agent was born. *Charles-Geneviève d'Eon* was initiated in the dangerous mysteries of the «King's Secret», Louis XV's personal network of information. He – or she... stretched the simulation so far that no one every really knew if they were dealing with a man or a woman. In both cases there were plenty of adventures, including amorous ones: Beaumarchais asked for her – or his... hand in marriage! Much better than James Bond! *Alfred Grévin* was born nearby, at Epineuil. His drawings were his best works: sarcastic and not at all foolish, the inventor of the wax museum is also a Burgundian. An amusing *civic museum* tells the whole story.

But what really strikes one about Tonnerre is the attention given to the poor. The **Hospital**, built in the XIIIth century by Margaret of Burgundy, widow of Charles d'Anjou, King of Naples and brother of Saint Louis, consists of an immense nave with oak vaults. This building was built for forty patients. Note the *«Mise au tombeau»*, a wonderful composition in XVth century Flemish Burgundy style. Dream in front of the **Fosse Dionne**. This is a karst spring the source of which is located far away. Celtic soldiers and Roman legions drank from it. It was turned into a wash-house in the XVIIIth century. Not a lot of bad things have been uttered about this pool: it was said that a snake lived in its green waters.

(Left) The Fosse Dionne; (below) the "Mise au Tombeau" by Jean de la Sonette.

(Left) Place du Marché au Blé; (right) the "Porte Piente" and the entrance to the town.

NOYERS

You can stop here. A hard task for the modern traveller worried about missing the seventh capital of the transept of the Collegiate Church of Saint-Eusèbe, whose formal audacity has been revealed to him by learned works... Too much running from one monument to another, with your nose in the air, can mean that you pass by something important. For example, the sculptor of the seventh capital certainly did not create it in order to «astonish tourists». He was paid – and rather badly as far as we know – to shape the stone. The second the monk-architect turned his back the workman's chisel flew. An angel or a demon was created out of the limestone. God would receive it in the most fitting way. On Judgement Day the anonymous creator would have at least this piece of work to redeem his poor life: *a stone image*. What has curiosity got to do with all of this?

Say out loud some of the street names of Noyers: *La Petite Etape aux vins (Little Halting-place of Wines), Le Poids du Roy (The King's Weight), Le Marché au Blé (The Corn Market), Le Grenier à Sel (The Salt Barn), La Porte Peinte (The Painted Door)...* in another place I know of someone who lives at: Salvador-Allende group, block 9, cage 37. Cage... free men, maybe the last ones, live at Noyers. If you want to see the town from the top of the bell-tower of the Notre-Dame Church, you have to ask for the keys from the Town Hall. From there you will be able to see the walls of the sixteen rounded towers, contained within the meanders of the river Serein, wooden structured houses resting on deep cellars and, past Saint-Parabin Square, the Burgundy of vineyards and forests, which lives following the rhythms of the seasons.

A miracle which has been preserved.

TANLAY

The splendid *castle* of Tanlay, preceded by a Louis XIII triumphal arch, is a Renaissance residence which was completed in the XVIIth century. Take the time to begin from the gardens and park which were planned around a large canal.

The castle has had a contrasting history. It was begun by François de Coligny, one of the leaders of the Protestant party in the XVIth century during the Religious Wars and brother of the «Amiral» assassinated on the night of Saint Bartholomew, to the sound of the bells of Saint-Germain l'Auxerrois... The elders of the Reformation used to meet in the *League tower*. The décor was rather strange for such a serious assembly. The dome is decorated by a fresco in an Italianized style of the Fontainebleau School, depicting characters from the court of Henry II, in the clothes and with the very light attributes of Mars, Juno and Venus...

Michel Particelli of Hemery, Cardinal Mazzarino's revenue officer, finished Tanlay castle. He was a bit heavy handed – probably in order to help him finish his palace. The taxpayers who were crushed by his revenues composed reproachful satires about the cardinal. «They sing, they pay...» said the minister. He did not, however, forget the old precautionary measure of many rulers: to sacrifice a «scapegoat». And this scapegoat was the revenue officer who was a naturalized native of Burgundy. Tanlay is a private residence which is tastefully inhabited. Not only shadows are evoked in the *Vestibule of Caesars*. The renewed gesture of the old is humanized by the surroundings of trees and water. Burgundy has subtly measured the audacity of this exotic marvel.

14

ANCY-LE-FRANC

There is a *Hall of Caesars* to welcome you here as well. But none of the rather conventional and detached reverence of old tastes: the whole of Ancy-le-Franc is an Italian palace.

Antoine de Clermont, Count of Tonnerre, the son of a nobleman from Delphi who became Burgundian by means of a happy marriage, always an advisable way of obtaining naturalization... Grand-Maître of the Waters and Forests, Lieutenant-General of Delphi, brother-in-law of the justly renowned Diane de Poitier, mistress of King Henry II – nineteen years her junior... – was a very prominent personage. In 1546 he began building a castle of regal dimensions. The work took more than half a century to complete, and always respected the initial idea.

The architect was *Sebastiano Serlio* of Bologna. Although his theoretical works are well known, there are hardly any other examples of his creations. He had to work respecting – and this is an interesting link – Burgundy's feudal tradition: this square building stands on a terrace surrounded by a ditch, which presently can only be imagined until it is dug out again; the building is surrounded by four corner towers; four doors, once preceded by drawbridges, give access to the central courtyard. This courtyard has the miraculous charm of the country residence of a «Gonfalonier of the Holy Roman Church». There is a touch of genius in the dialogue between the round niches and the pillars of the Corinthian capitals: this is the «rhythmic arch» which *Bramante* imagined for the Vatican... The stairs have been relegated to the extremities of the structures in order to give the Italian-style continuity of internal volumes. The *Primaticcio* and *Niccolò dell'Abbate* painted the vaults, depicting gods and heroes.

In the Medea Gallery you can follow the Argonauts sailing towards Colchis. You will hear more about the *Golden Fleece...*

(Left): Two views of the castle of Tanlay.　　　　　*The castle of Ancy-le-Franc by Serlio.*

CHATILLON-SUR-SEINE

North west Burgundy – with its powerful cities, princely vineyards and Italian buildings – is the pleasant, flowered and royal route to the Ile-de-France. It is, however, possible to choose the north road through Champagne. In this case the first place to stop off in Burgundy is Châtillon, near the source of the Seine. Here *Saint Bernard* studied the humanities. You can discover the town from the hill on which the **Church of Saint-Vorles** is siutated. Châtillon was devastated several times by hordes. It was here that in 1914 Joffre wrote the agenda of the *Battle of Marne*: «In the moment in which a battle is undertaken which shall determine the destiny of our country...»

The **Museum** is very exciting. In 1953 a secondary school teacher discovered the *tomb of the Princess of Vix*. For 2500 years a young woman, who it is known was beautiful and who it is thought was blond, was buried in a parade coach, at the gates of Châtillon, crowned with a gold tiara. She was surrounded by works of art of rare beauty – Etruscan, Greek, Scythian – including the biggest *bronze crater* left to us from Ancient times. A frieze of horsemen is the mysterious sign of the exchange.

The mysterious Vix tomb: (above) a rare photograph of the reconstruction of the parade coach the wooden elements of which have been lost. (Below) the Scythian gold tiara belonging to the Princess.

16

View of a Burgundian canal.

THE CANALS

The *Vix tomb* shows the determining importance of waterways throughout Burgundy's history. We do not know the name, the language, nor the gods of this people which – in the VIth century B.C. – was able to offer a young woman this extraordinary viaticum of European masterpieces for her final journey. They settled at the point in which the river becomes navigable. The caravans which had crossed the snow-topped Alps and Jura, placed worked metals, woollen drapes and ceramics on the wharfs and loaded up with tin from the British Isles, amber from the banks of the Baltic and linen from the northern plains. In the evenings, by the fireside, the mule-drivers from Styria and the miners from Cornwall, the gunsmiths from Volterra and the waste wax melters from Corinth, attempted to make frinds. Behind the «barred spur» of dry stones of their proud fortress, the Lords of Halstatt surrounded a sacred vergin, with terrifying reverence...

The rivers lead out of Burgundy: the Seine, Loire, Saône and Rhône... Men carrying goods, laden horses on Celtic ridge trails, carts passing along the Roman roads, the expert presence of merchants and middlemen, the toll and protection of gentlemen, the refuge and solace of the sanctuaries led, over thousands of years, to the development of the Burgundy crossroads. Undoubtedly the dreadful service on offer was very expensive. Finding a way to connect the rivers was a great ambition from the beginning of the XVIth century. This ambition was fulfilled in the XVIIIth century. The «Etats de Bourgogne» – the regional Assembly at that time – was so satisfied by the immense work carried out that in 1788 it erected an obelisk at Dijon as a sign of «eternal» gratitude to Louis XVI...

Burgundy has over 1.200 kilometres of navigable waterways, covering the region in every direction. It is possible to travel on a cruise boat or hire a houseboat. This is a wonderful, maybe the best, way to discover this untouched land. In the evening, after mooring the boat, you can choose between a welcoming inn and the «Table d'hôte» of a farm. Now you can understand how, in the midst of the foolish arrogance of modern cuisine and the horrible smell of burnt fat of the «fast food» chains, it is still possible for a meal to become a feast.

(Above) the porter's lodge; (below) a general plan of the abbey.

FONTENAY

(Above right) The main body of the abbey (XVIIIth century); (below) the dove-cot.

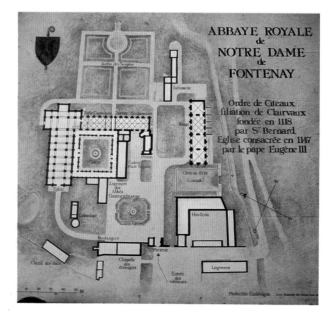

ABBAYE ROYALE
de
NOTRE DAME
de
FONTENAY

Ordre de Cîteaux
filiation de Clairvaux
fondée en 1118
par St Bernard
Eglise consacrée en 1147
par le pape Eugène III

This is definetely a unique monument. More than a masterpiece of Romanesque art, it is the only remaining monastery in the world built according to the will of *Saint Bernard*. This monastery was built following a concept of rigour and passion, which is well expressed in this verse from the Psalm of David: « *What is there for me in heaven and what could I desire on earth, if not You?* ». In the heart of a forest crossed by clear waters, stands an ideal town where the stones themselves are a prayer. Whilst you look distractedly at the buildings in the first courtyard: the porter's lodge, the guest-rooms, and the service lodgings, I would like to tell you a couple of things about the Cistercian Order, Saint Bernard and God's Love. We make a great effort to understand the people who built Borobodour, the mosque of El Aqsa or the temple of Kyoto, so why not do the same thing here? Even though we were born in the West, in a society which preserves vague references to Christianity, nothing can prepare us for our encounter with Fontenay.

At the end of the XIth century – when the powerful order of Saint Benedict, founded at Cluny in Burgundy, reigned over the Europe of prayer – some monks decided to *return to the desert*. They considered the black Order to be too safe, too solid and too rich. They applied these words of the Lord to the Order: « *If at least I had found you to be hot or cold! But since I have found you to be tepid, I*

will vomit you from my mouth». The dissidents decided to settle in the Low Countries of Burgundy, in the humid and muddy forest broken by rare clearings and secret pools surrounded by armfuls of reeds, the «cistels»: at *Citeaux*.

The Cistercians dressed in white as a sign of disunion: white is the natural colour of wool and it was thus unnecesary for it to be dyed and starched as was the case when preparing the drapes of the Benedictine cowls. The community decided to decline the profits from revenue, benefices and feudal rights and organize itself around work: nobody excluded. The monks, who were mostly priests, were assisted by *lay brothers*, and specialists in forging, carpentry and stabling. But the elected Abbot led only his fellow brothers – monks and lay brothers – in the heaviest work: tilling, ploughing, and harvesting. Just imagine what the implements and yield were like in those times... The Saxon Saint Etienne Harding gave them another mission: to establish, with the help of the Holy Rabbis, the original text of the Bible and illustrate it with painted visions, representing one of the most interesting and baffling displays of Romanesque art. They also got up in the middle of the night to sing: «*The voice of the turtle-dove has been heard on this Earth...*».

Their madness had turned them into «a handful of sick and poor» when, in April 1111, around thirty men – we shall not call them «noblemen» because this term would be anachronistic, but certainly they were «chevaliers», that class of men who lived by the glory of the sword – knocked on their door. These men were headed by *Bernard de Fontaine*, whose father was an officer of the Duke of Burgundy and whose mother was a saint. The Order of Citeaux began a wonderful adventure. During Bernard's lifetime alone, 328 monasteries were founded all over Europe. They subsequently became over a thousand.

The community's church: rigour and light.

(Above right) The monks' dormitory; (below) Our Lady of Fontenay.

There follows just some basic information about *Saint Bernard*, the last «Doctor of the Church». Abbot of Clairvaux – on the border between Champagne and Burgundy – promoter of the reconquest of souls, he dictated violent instructions to Popes and Kings, in which his deep contempt for the world emerged. He led the purest – and most unlucky – of the Crusades to save the Christian Kingdom in the Holy Land which he had endowed with an inspired army: the *Order of the Temple*. He hated money, vanity, anti-Semitism and compromise: figures of the Devil in front of which the modern world would bow down. A witness said: «Whenever he preached in public or in private, mothers would hide their children, wives would hold back their husbands, and friends would stop their friends from going to hear him, because the Holy Spirit instilled such power in his words that any feelings of the heart could not have held back some of those who listened to him». He himself said to his brothers: «When we pray together, do you not also often feel your bowels deeply stirred by the memory of the joy awaiting us in the Jerusalem of the heavens, our mother? During that meditation our faces are covered in tears. Oh! If only it could last!».

Of the multitude of abbeys he created, Bernard had two favourites: *Claire Vallée* – Clairvaux – his earthly abode, built in the gloomy valley of Champagne, a land of absinth and reptiles; and the *Val des Sources* – Fontenay – in the land of his mother. The great church of Clairvaux was demolished and the monastery rebuilt in the XVIIIth century, with ostentatious faithlessness; then this luminous monastery was transformed into the worst of

(Above) The capitular room opening onto the cloister.

(Right) The cloister, symbolic centre of the world.

On the following page: two views of the water driven forge.

prisons: a sewer for hardened criminals... *Fontenay*, however, is still standing and is almost intact.

In 1119, a group of thirteen monks from Clairvaux founded the first retreat in the forest. Slightly further down the valley stood the Abbey whose altar was consecrated in 1147 by Pope Eugene III, Bernard's Cistercian disciple. Fontenay owes not only its layout, but also its beauty to the Abbot of Clairvaux himself.

The rules of the Order situated around the *cloister* – the symbolic centre of the world – the *church* dedicated to prayer and contemplation, the *capitular room* for informal homiles and the governing of souls, the *dormitories* for the monks and lay brothers as resting-places for exhausted bodies, the *book house* for meditation and the tireless work of reproducing the Scriptures, and the *forge* and *workrooms* where advanced techniques made it possible to save God's time. All of this surrounded by a *wall*. This barrier isolating the monastery was not conceived in order to stop anybody from going out. For example, the Cistercians did not decline the work of Preaching. Saint Bernard, «exhausted and already marked by death», preached from Flanders to Italy, stirring the enthusiasm of the crusading princes under Vézelay, and staggering the terrifying certainties of the first Catharists in Languedoc. This wall recreated the desert, the place quoted in the Word of God in which only those who have been called may enter.

The perfect and solemn harmony of Fontenay is due to the aesthetic concept of Saint Bernard who reflected and wrote a lot about religious art. He condemned flattering ornaments, excessive imagery, and spectacular repetition which debased the immense Romanesque gesture. He banished decorations, colours and sculptures. Even the *Image of Our Lady* – the much loved Vergin – was not allowed in the church... Bernard left the architects with eternal materials: *space and light*.

He also said: «If we think of this wall not as a collection of stones, but as the Communion of Saints, we will see that any breaches in the wall are the spaces left by dethroned angels; we know very well that these places should be filled by men: *the ruins must be rebuilt using living stones*.

ALESIA

A Roman electoral campaign was concluded here...
Julius Caesar, a demagogic aristocrat, contemptuous of
his class and people, felt that the great offices of the
Republic were slipping away from him, and so he decided
to entrust himself with the conquest of Gaul. He took
advantage of the internal divisions of the Celtic towns
and the anxiety of the Aedui – the inhabitants of
Burgundy at that time – in the face of the threatened
Helvetian invasion, and marched his legions northwards.
His objective – such are the deviations of politics – was in
the south: Rome and power.

In order for the eagle's victory to appear more
spectacular, it was necessary to make the Gauls appear
rich and barbaric. They were neither of these things: good
fathers, devoted to a well-developped agriculture, they
invented the barrel, the combine harvester and salted
meat. They conveyed to France their patience, their taste
for debate and the name of the skylark. They were
without doubt better than their conquerors because they
had just got rid of their «war kings» and believed in one
God. But Caesar was a splendid writer: his bulletins,
collected in his *Commentaries* which have been
devotedly deciphered by generations of schoolchildren,
gave the idea of a dangerous Gaul, populated by wild
blond-haired giants, intent on counting the gold from
their sackings amidst human sacrifices... this nonsense
won him votes in the *Forum*. In 52 B.C., the Roman
managed to lock up the leader of a revolt which was
almost a national movement in the oppidan of *Alésia*.
Vercingétorix was strangled and, not long afterwards, so
was the Republic of Rome.

(Above) Vercingétorix, statue erected by Napoleon III.
(Below) the Gaul-Roman town.

BUSSY-RABUTIN

Another Versailles, of nostalgic dimensions, built by an exile, against his will: this is Burgundy's most touching castle.

Roger de Rabutin, Count of Bussy, whose cradle was surrounded by all the fairies. «General camp master of the light cavalry», well-endowed in matters of love, war and songs he was, however, born too late. In the reign of Louis XIII, he would have been a fantastic companion of the «Three Musketeers», fencing with the Cardinal's guards, impudently holding the chair of the Académie Française, leaving the Queen's ladies-in-waiting with sweet memories yet never making any of them suffer... his misfortune was that Louis XIV was desperately lacking in imagination.

During an important Court Ball, the Sun-King was carried away by the music of the violins of Lulli. *Madame de Sévigné*, out of breath after having danced with the King, fell back into an armchair, fanning herself, and said to Roger de Rabutin, her relation: «Oh, my dear cousin, we have a great King!». Her cousin did not share this view for very long... An epigram, in the old fashioned style, about the King's loves, and an even more irreverent «*Histoire amoureuse des Gaules*» – the chronicle with a key of a power which fell into ridicule by acting freely and demanding respect – cost him first a temporary exile, then the Bastille and finally – in 1666 – permanent confinement in his homeland of Burgundy. Roger who was handsome and still young, was excluded from Versailles. At first he received friends, then inopportune

visitors, and then scroungers... One day, he found himself alone: the risk of doing something considered unwelcome, the muddy roads, the mediocre quality of the meat had discouraged everybody.

So Roger de Rabutin made his castle an enchanted kingdom. Under his personal direction, travelling painters, industrious craftsmen and shrewd scholars transformed the old feudal fortress, lightened in the XVIth century by a Renaissance-style façade opening onto the park. Renowned captains, splendid women, and derisive allegories surrounded his solitude. Discover the charm of the ensembles in the *antechamber of men of war*, the *hall of uniforms*, and the *golden tower*. It is also important to listen to the details. With the right amout of anger necessary to be lucid, a witness recalls the shadows of the Great Age, the bitterness of the isolation and the coin of glory. By chance there is this written under the portrait of a lady whose charms are less striking than her certain air of benevolence: «*Madame de... less well known for her beauty than for the use she made of it*».

When Roger de Rabutin went out onto his terrace – oh! those so orderly rows of apple trees delimiting the walk of a horseman born for the attack... – he could contemplate the village of *Bussy-Le-Grand* inhabited by rather poor vine-dressers. A century later, *Andoche Junot* was born there, a strange and admirable soldier of the Revolution and the Empire. His old father would proudly sign thus the sale of some parts of his vineyard: «Andoche Junot, *father of the Duke of Abrantès...*».

(Left) Complete view of the castle of Bussy-Rabutin.

Roger de Rabutin in the Hall of Uniforms and amidst the Men of War.

EPOISSES

Guillaume de Pechpeyrou-Comminges de Guitaut was extraordinarily handsome. In 1661 he became, by alliance, the owner of the marquisate and the residence of Epoisses. Thus an illustrious family from Quercy took root in Burgundy, and remained there with rare distinction.

A fortress stood here in the VIth century. It was here that *Brunehaut* confronted Saint Colomban who refused to bless the bastard child of his son, Thierry. The old Queen of Austrasia, who was tied to the tail of a wild horse by her young rival, was much loved in Burgundy. For a long time the stone tracks of the Celts and the paved Roman roads were still called *Brunehaut's roads*. They were certainly good times because – going against common sense – it was claimed that the bloodthirsty queen paid a lot of attention to public works.

The Dukes of Burgundy wanted the castle – which was begun in the Xth century – to always remain in good hands. During the Classical Period it was one of the top provincial houses. *Madame de Sévigné* visited it. 76 of her «castle letters» have been preserved: «I want to announce to you the most unthinkable, the most extraordinary, the most surprising piece of news...». During the Revolution, the lord of the castle's sister having emigrated, the Popular Committees razed half of the buildings to the ground. That gave Epoisses a lot of free space towards the village. And anyway, half a folly is always better than a whole one.

A special type of *cheese* is made in the village. Recently, a guide-book claimed that «the aroma could be recognized within a range of a hundred leagues». Since one league is about 4 kilometres, this seems a bit exaggerated. It is, however, true that the cheese does have a very powerful smell.

The part of the castle which survived the Revolution.

A town which comes straight out of medieval miniatures.

SEMUR

Semur-en-Auxois, or *love at first sight*! This marvellously preserved and lively town has kept the appearance of a «country» capital. The town stands inside its walls which dominate the clear waters of the Armaçon, just like the radiant towns of medieval miniatures, in the centre of a natural region with a charming personality.

Auxois was rich. For centuries an intelligent balance reigned there. Cultivation and grasslands were alternated; the meadows themselves were divided into the arid hillside pastures and the fertile «fattening» lands of the valleys; forging, weaving, and brilliant craftwork diversified the town's resources. The main type of breeding – at least according to the spirit of the community – was basically that of *horses*. In the Middle Ages the horse was the instrument of combat that also made it possible to increase agricultural yield: in both cases, horses were a sign of power and modernity. Up until the last war, the inhabitants of Auxois were proud of their irreplaceable rôle as «energy suppliers»: the strongest colts went to form the great draugh-horses of the plains and cereal-growing plateaux, the more tractable colts cut furrows between the rows of stumps on the Hills, or transported timber from the forests. The mechanization of agriculture led to the disappearance of the economic rôle of the horse and yet all of the suburbs of Auxois still organize their annual *stud mare* competition.

Some – *Allerey*, for example – organize draught and racing trials and since back in 1639, every year on the 31st May at Semur, the *Ring Race* is held, the oldest race in France, with the prize being a ring of the town's arms. The breeding of bovines has been increased. Burgundy has its own breed: the white *Charolais* – a characteristic feature of the landscape of pasture-land. This breed is reared in meadows and produces a meat of excellent quality. Competition from the mass-imported «hormone-filled zebus» is strong...

The **town of Semur** has preserved its appearance of a XIVth and XVth century fortress, when it was one of the most powerful fortified towns in the duchy, able to withstand the English Royal army. The towers: *Orle d'or (Gold barrier), Gehenne, Prison* and *Margot* are particularly impressive when seen from the *Pont Joly*, which crosses the Armaçon to the west. By following the base of the town-walls it is possible to climb up again along the pink granite slope and enter the town. A beautiful tree-covered walk dominating the valley leads back southwards to the church whose two square towers command the view.

The **church of Notre-Dame** is a good example of a triple-erected Gothic church, introduced in Burgundy at the beginning of the XIIIth century and originated in the workrooms of Picardie, l'Ile-de-France and Champagne. The apse – in the gardens of the town hall – is of a great

The ramparts of Pont Joly.

(Right) A bend of the Armaçon.

purity. The XVth century vestibule was seriously mutilated during the Revolution. In fact, at that time Semur had a particularly violent «patriotic club». The nave, tall and narrow, is a brilliant exercise in architecture, greatly admired by Viollet-le-Duc. Worth seeing in the chapels of the left side nave are the «*Mise au Tombeau*» (Sepulchre) in the Burgundy-Flemish tradition of the Carthusian monastery of Champmol and, above all, the «*Vitraux des métiers*», the sequence of stained glass windows depicting the trades. Initially, in the Middle Ages, the professions were organized in religious brotherhoods under the protection of a patron saint, in order to guarantee assistance and mutual aid. These were progressively transformed into «trades» to ensure professional training and a respect for quality regulations. Much later the royal powers turned them into «guilds», which were then abolished by the Revolution. The stained glass windows of Semur date back to the XVth century, a satisfactory and joyous period. Some elements of the *Chapel of the Butchers and Delicatessens* still remain and, more importantly, the complete cycle, comprised of eight panels, of the *Drapers' Chapel*. This last series is of exceptional documentary interest in Europe. It opportunely emphasizes the strength of urban industry in medieval Burgundy. Semur was neither Bruges nor Florence. However, top quality cloths were made from the wool obtained from the large flocks of sheep of the abbeys and rural communities. The

same goes for Châtillon, Dijon and Beaune... This command of techniques justified other ambitions.

An ancient chronicle declares that the inhabitants of Semur are pleasant people «*who like to meet foreigners*». In effect, this is a pleasant town to visit especially by foot. There is a charming **museum**: the Corots were kindly repatriated by Japanese collectors who had been offered them by unscrupulous people; there is a *library* which includes, amongst its other treasures, the *Missal of Anne of Brittany*; there is an adorable **theatre** in which it is possible to imagine Madame de Rénal trying not to look towards the stalls at the handsome face of Julien Sorel... There are some important classical constructions: old convents and magistrates' buildings which only offer the high vestibules and dignified gates of prohibited retreats. The *Marchioness of Chatelet*, a dear friend of Voltaire, and wife of the governor of Semur, lived in one of these buildings.

Semur is a paradise for two singular types of artist: connoisseurs of furniture and old books and cinematographers. Auctions, galleries and antique shops greet the former. The image artists are first of all seduced by the overall picture, and then charmed by the intact soul of an astonishing town. I remember when an adaptation of «Affaire Blaireau» by Alphonse Allais was being filmed: *Ni vu, ni connu* by Yves Robert. The hero was a poacher with a golden heart, played by Louis de Funès. It was not possible to follow the shooting schedule:

the gendarmes turned their noses up at the scenario; the communicants did not look sufficiently absorbed; the «old men» convened for repeated libations lost all dignity at the fifth take... that evening, on the terrace of one of the old houses in the city walls, the crew gathered around an *aligoté*. Then Louis de Funès talked to us about the town, before Danièle Delorme's radiant smile. Semur or love at first sight!

One of the roads to Dijon passes through **Saint-Thibaut**, 20 kilometres to the south-west of Semur. This is an inspired place. In the XIVth century the English burnt everything down. All that remains of the church is a sculpted *portal* and the bright *choir* of the new sanctuary, the construction of which was started in the florid XVth century. This town is a marvel lost in the typical landscape of meadows bordered by bright hedges. Touching and discreet pilgrims go there to honour Saint Thibaut: the last followers of the *Petite Eglise*, hostile to the Pope who came to a compromise with Bonaparte in 1801.

(Above left) Two views of the church of Notre-Dame; (below) the XVIth century "Mise au Tombeau".

(Right) The "Porte Sauvigny", main entrance of the old town; (below) road with wooden structured houses.

DIJON

An enigmatic town, attractive and reserved. A town it takes time to learn to love.

For twelve centuries Dijon was a cheerful, rural capital of no more than 20.000 inhabitants. Today it is the centre of an economic agglomerate of 230.000 inhabitants. The XIXth century should have harmonized the valuable acquisitions of the past with the modern-day developments. Unfortunately, mediocre local council administrations were not able to make this combination. The medieval and classical historic centre, the original meeting place of the valleys, the spirit of the town marked by a shadowy particularism were denied: for example, the Holy Ducal Chapel was destroyed, the vineyards on the hills around Dijon were parcelled off, the town-planning scheme of Paris was copied. This contradiction carried on for a long time: the last absurd «penetrations» into the older quarters, the plundering of tree-covered squares, the building of the University outside the town, only go back to the XXth century... Thus growth meant rupture and a kind of uneasiness remains. The risk is there, a challenge for tomorrow's leaders. The inhabitants of Dijon have not been affected too much, but it has become rather difficult to understand their town.

In order to get to know Dijon, it is necessary to have the power of *Asmodeus*, the naïve demon, who discovered concealed dwellings and hidden lives. Thus, in the buildings and houses built between «courtyards and gardens» – and not along the roads, maybe that is actually the secret... – it is possible to feel the intact heartbeat of one of the most surprising towns of the West. Not everybody is granted this *demon's-eye view*, especially visitors who only remain a few hours. But there is quite an accessible possibility. Just climb the 316 steps of the **Tower of Philip the Good**, at the centre of the ducal palace. For me this is an indispensable initiation. The terrace opens onto all four horizons: the western threshold of crossings and shelters, the northern plateau from which the Seine descends, the eastern valley with the languid Saône at the feet of the bluish Jura mountains, and the «purple and gold» hills running southwards. See how the town reassembles itself around its bell-towers, how the suburbs gather aorund the free land of the abbeys, and how the new quarters extend along the paths of communication and exchange...

In the VIth century, *Grégoire de Tours*, found the town of Dijon almost unchanged from the original modest Gaul-Roman *castrum*: «*Dijon has four entrances, directed towards the four points of the heavens. The walls are adorned by thirty-three towers which are built in freestone up to a height of twenty feet... On the western side there are fertile mountains covered in vines.*» The good bishop noted that these vineyards produced «*such a noble Falernian wine that the inhabitants had no esteem at all for the wine of Ascalon*». The reference to wines of classical ancientry is just made to cover up his amazement. He saw the windmills turning along the waterways of the Ouche, the Raines and the Suzon and the joyful activities of a courteous and very religious

The capital of Burgundy seen from the Ducal Tower.

people. In the chaos of Franco-Europe, his stay at Dijon was like a breath of fresh air.

The Capetian dukes of Burgundy, the race of iron that took the throne of the Fleurs-de-lis in 1031 and held on to it, surviving to the oldest ramification, chose Dijon as their capital. They played a prominent rôle in important medieval events and in the encounter with the East: two dukes and one of their sons died during a Crusade, one duke dreamed of being King of Thessalonica, another one refused the crown of Jerusalem, a cadet created the dynasty and kingdom of Portugal, another became Prince of Morée, and another Pope. The lord of their castle of *Fontaine*, Tescelin le Roux, gave his own son to Citeaux: he became *Saint Bernard*. At the end of the XIIth century, Dijon was granted liberties which it jealously maintained for a long time to come: the «town corps» was led by a *viscount major* who exercised the right of justice and never permitted anyone to display any lack of respect for the same.

The second generation dukes – XIVth and XVth centuries – owe everything to the genius of their founder *Philip the Hardy* – son of the battle of Poitiers: «Father, careful to the right, to the left...» – and his happy marriage to *Marguerite de Male*, heiress to the counties of Flanders, Artois and the part of Burgundy beyond the Saône later called «franco». *John the Fearless, Philip the Good, Charles* – who the French called «the Bold» – were all born in the old palace of Dijon. The *Holy Chapel* was the seat of the *Golden Fleece*, the order of chivalry which ran the Burgundy-Flemish state; at the town-gates, the *Carthusian monastery of Champmol* invented new art forms around the ducal necropolis; it was impossible to know who to admire most amongst the bourgeois of the town: the salt shareholders, the goldsmiths, the spur-makers... In January 1477 a young woman learnt of the collapse of a dream. A few days earlier, the herald announced the following words to her father, which resounded like the fanfares of a lost Europe: «Charles, by the grace of God, Duke of Burgundy, of Lothier, of Brabant, of Limbourg, of Luxemburg and of Gueldre, Count of Flanders, Artois and Burgundy, Palatine of Hainaut, Holland, Zealand and Namur, Marquis of the Holy Empire, Lord of Frise, Salins and Malines.» And suddenly there was silence... in order to preserve the heritage, *Mary of Burgundy* gave herself to Maximilian of Habsburg. Another adventure began in which Dijon played no part. After the entry of the French troops, the last «master builder of the duke's works», *Antoine le Moiturier*, was seen roaming the streets of the town, begging for a crust of bread...

The royal powers paid a lot of attention to Dijon. At least they gave this impression... For a long time they distrusted the sentiments of the people. Since the *County* had fought against Louis XI for its independence – and was happy to remain that way – the *Duchy* had become a border province. On the other side of the Saône reigned the blood of the old dynasty... Certainly Dijon defended itself, for example in 1513 against the Swiss and later against the imperial forces, because all these armies bore increasingly less resemblance to the heirs to the power of Burgundy. However, risings broke out easily: on 26th June 1477, *Chrétiennot Vyon* stirred up the town to the shout

The wing of the "Etats".

The "Logis du Roi" and the tower of the Great Dukes of the West.

of «Long live Madame Marie!»; on 27th February 1630, *Antoine Changenet* led a group of vine-dressers who entered the higher quarters of the town to the mocking cry of *Lanturelu*, mixed with subversive calls of «Long live the Emperor!»... Louis XIII entered Dijon through the breach, preceded by gunners *ready to fire*; Louis XI did not dare to venture beyond the Gate of Saint-Nicolas: very little progress had been made in one and a half centuries.

Burgundy had accepted the annexation with France, with some important restrictions. At the «Etats-Généraux» of 1484, the captain of justice, *Philippe Pot*, pronounced these famous words: «*The monarchy is a dignity not a prince's property... The delegates of the three States are the depositaries of the will of everybody.*» At the «Etats Généraux» of 1789, Dijon only sent delegates who were firmly resolved to demand the respect of these principles: they were all to the left of the national Assembly... In the meantime, the Orders: clergy, nobility and middle classes, had more or less maintained their financial power. Dijon did not accept everything that the monarchy wanted: in 1572, for example, on the night of Saint Bartholomew, the *Count of Chabot-Charny* refused to carry out the order to massacre the Protestants.

Three centuries of centralized monarchic power did not end all that badly. The King had the good idea of making Dijon a judicial capital. The headquarters of the *Audit Office* had always been located here. Louis XI added the supreme court: the *Parliament* was snatched away from Beaune, an indomitable town which had tried to defend «the freedom and privileges of Burgundy» with the use of weapons. This meant the creation of a haughty, rich and cultured class which gave the town a tone of austere dignity. The noble, somewhat cold, parliamentary buildings make a beautiful sight, but they are more than this: in 1780, the *Bouhier* library, created by nine generations of magistrates, held 31.652 printed volumes and 2.010 ancient manuscripts... Naturally, the *men in red* dominated the states of the province.

In 1678 Louis XVI annexed the County to France. Burgundy was no longer a border line and rediscovered the brothers from which it had been separated. The King had the architect of Versailles, *Mansart*, rebuild all the southern parts of the ducal palace, which now opened onto a huge hemicycled square. In his new *residence*, the King had himself depicted in the garments of the *conqueror of the Golden Fleece*... The prince of Condé, hereditary governor of Burgundy, stayed there occasionally. He was surrounded by a rather varied army of volunteers. Six officials, thirty-three cavalrymen and twelve foot-soldiers, dressed in sumptuous uniforms, were his guard of honour. When the ceremonies ended the *Musketeer Guards of H.H. Monseigneur the Prince of Condé* went back to being notaries, tilers, butlers, innkeepers...

The representative assembly – the «*Etats*» – did not

(Above left) The stairway of the processions by Gabriel;
(below) the Hall of the "Etats" of Burgundy.

(Left) The "Tour de Bar"; (right) Claes Sluter
by H. Bouchard.

want to be inferior. They entrusted their own classical western wing to a pupil of Mansart's, built a refined *Chapel of the Elect* and had *Gabriel*, the architect of the Trianon, build a monumental stairway for the dignity of its processions. In effect, there were many processions at Dijon: for the «Mass of the Holy Spirit, the opening ceremony of the 'Etats'», *the Feast of the Sacred Host...* These stairways, galleries, huge halls and courtyards should be imagined swarming with immense crowds of people: delegates of the communes – not at all compelled to dress in black – sparkling noblemen wearing diamonds, crested according to the fashion of Versailles, bishops in every shade of violet and purple, representatives of the Audit Office in blue moire, presidents of parliament in red togas and triple ermine, «Muskateer Guards of Mgr» with their powdered hair and faces as red as their doublets. Plus large cordons, gold plaques of the orders decorated with doves, lace rochets... In the centre, a dark man, the *Superintendent*, preannouncing the power of tomorrow: that of anonyous offices. One day a singular procession crossed the **Place d'Armes**, still dominated by the «bronze horse» of the Great King's equestrian statue: some gloomy figures dressed in black advanced in *no particular order* – this was noted by witnesses – between savage guards... The municipal administration of 1790 entered the attack: in this way the astonished population of Dijon learnt that the Revolution had come about. Now you will understand why I advised you to go first of all to the heart of the town and its

history, to the *Tower of Duke Philip*. You should now go along to the **Palace of the Dukes**: the «Fortified House» of the Counts in dark times, the castle and sanctuary of the first generation dukes, the palace of the «Great Dukes of the West», royal Residence and seat of the provincial «Etats». In the northern wing, where the Dukes of Valois lived, the high XVth century façades dominate the *Dukes' garden*. The palace opens onto the *«traders'»* *quarter*, around *Notre-Dame du Marché*: Coppersmiths, Glass-makers, Basket-makers, Blacksmiths Streets... This quarter extends eastwards with the *Tour de Bar* where *King René* who wanted to be crowned King of Naples, Lorraine, Anjou and Provence was held prisoner for a long time; and the *duke's kitchens, the Holy Chapel, and the Guards' Room* which you will soon discover in the museum. To the south, there are the classical façades of the *Logis du Roi* and the *Palais des Etats*. Visit the Chapel of the Elect; climb Gabriel's stairway to the hall where the solemn meetings of the assembly of Burgundy were held. Try and imagine all of these places alive: there is nothing colder than a theatre when the footlights have been switched off... Above all, remember that the *Parliamentary* quarters were situated in this wing: the halls of justice and magistrates' palaces. Here is a synthesis of the history: to the north the cheerful, trading town of the craftsmen, to the south the cold and imperious quarters of the pettifoggers. From Dukes to Kings the power – including the building symbolizing it – ended up by turning the wrong way...

The Museum of Fine Arts

Built in the XIXth century on the site of the Holy Chapel, this museum encompasses various ancient parts of the ducal palace. Access is through a square containing a statue of *Jean-Philippe Rameau* (1683-1764). The son of the organist of Notre-Dame du Marché, trained in a town which in the XVIIIth century had not lost the tradition of the «Chapelle de Bourgogne», this son of Dijon created, in addition to the royal ballet-opera, another immense opera of which musicians today – especially in Great Britain – are rediscovering the extraordinary inventiveness. Dijon does not devote itself much to him, as though Salzburg would have been content to dedicate just a statue to Mozart...

The **Museum of Fine Arts** is wonderfully rich. From the «Quattrocento» to Nicolas de Stael it gives an almost complete panorama of European art – with many masterpieces. We will talk later about its strongest moments linked to the history of Burgundy. But time must be taken to discover this museum, not between one visit and another, but as the only object of our attention.

The visit should be completed by going to the **Magnin National Museum** situated nearby in «Rue des Bons-Enfants». The name evokes the «domination» of the dukes, and it is famous for its drawings of mainly Italian origin.

(Left) The tower of Philip the Good; (below) Place d´"Armes" (de la Libération).

(Right) Rue des Forges.

The heart of the museum is regret.

Philip the Hardy, Duke of Burgundy, and *Gian Galeazzo Visconti*, Duke of Milan, together decided to ask the Pope for the privilege of building a «double Carthusian monastery» to house the tombs of the princes of their dynasty. Twenty-four white monks of the order of hermits, which had made seclusion their only joy: «*O beata solitudo, o sola beatitudo...*», would pray unrelentingly for those whose human fight had been without repose. It was a sublime idea to submit the dangerous actions of the State and war not only to the judgement of God, but also to the charity of the communion of saints... Thus at the end of the XIVth century, the **Carthusian monasteries** of *Pavia* and **Champmol** were erected. Today the monastery at Pavia shines, and that of Champmol is a mass of ruins...

How bright the future looked that day back in 1383 when *Jean Monsieur*, the boy who later became «Jean sans peur» (John the Fearless), laid the first Trinity stone near the Abbot's Pool, at the gates of Dijon. The Duke had summoned the architect of his brother, the King of France, to Dijon, together with glass and heald craftsmen from his brother's dominions in Berry, and sculptors and smelters from his States in Flanders. He ruined himself

On the opposite page: (above) Philip the Good by Roger van der Weyden; (below left) Jean-Philippe Rameau by Jacques-André Aved, (below right) Study for "Le Bal aux Folies-Bergères" by Edouard Manet.

Nativity by the Master of Flemalle.

The Guards' Hall: a romantic vision of the XIXth century.

(Right) The tombs at Champmol: (in the foreground) John the Fearless and Margaret of Baviera; (in the background) Philip the Hardy.

by buying Italian retablos and ancient ivories at the Court of the Pope at Avignon, the first examples of that prodigious art later known as «interior light» from the ateliers of Bruges, slabs of black marble from the quarries of Meuse and stones of alabaster from the quarries of Tuscany. A building yard was opened... for a century. «Image workers» from all over Europe chiselled angel's wings. The artistic currents were confused in a prolific dialogue. In the huge church, where the princes' tombs were to be placed, the altar was surmounted by the *polyptych of the Passion* by Simone Martini, a pupil of Duccio, and surrounded by huge gilded panels by Jacques de Baerze, on which Melchior Broderlam narrated the Infancy of Christ. In each of the twenty-four cells, a painting was offered for meditation: the *Great Round Pietà* by Jean Malouel, a *Vergin with Child* by Jan van Eyck...

Claes Sluter de Haarlem dominated the whole of the first period. He erected a *Calvary* at the centre of the main Cloister. It was a «Fountain of life»: a spring from which the powerful base of the Prophets carrying the Sacrificial Cross rose, this new fountain. Why was it necessary for an obtuse and disheartening stupidity to turn it into a «well»... He gathered the founder dukes and duchesses around the feet of the *Vergin* on the great portal of the Church. He supplied the solution for the *ducal tombs*, a composition of masses of unreal levity. His nephew, Claes de Werwe, Juan de la Huerta of Aragon, and the Frenchman Antoine le Moiturier finished his work. Together with them worked assistants and apprentices who learnt many lessons from them: thus, in nearly every church in Burgundy, we find these strong and gentle Vergins, with ample draping, carrying on their hips the Child destined to be sacrificed, still playing with a bunch of grapes... The *weeping* figures of their relatives accompanied Philip the

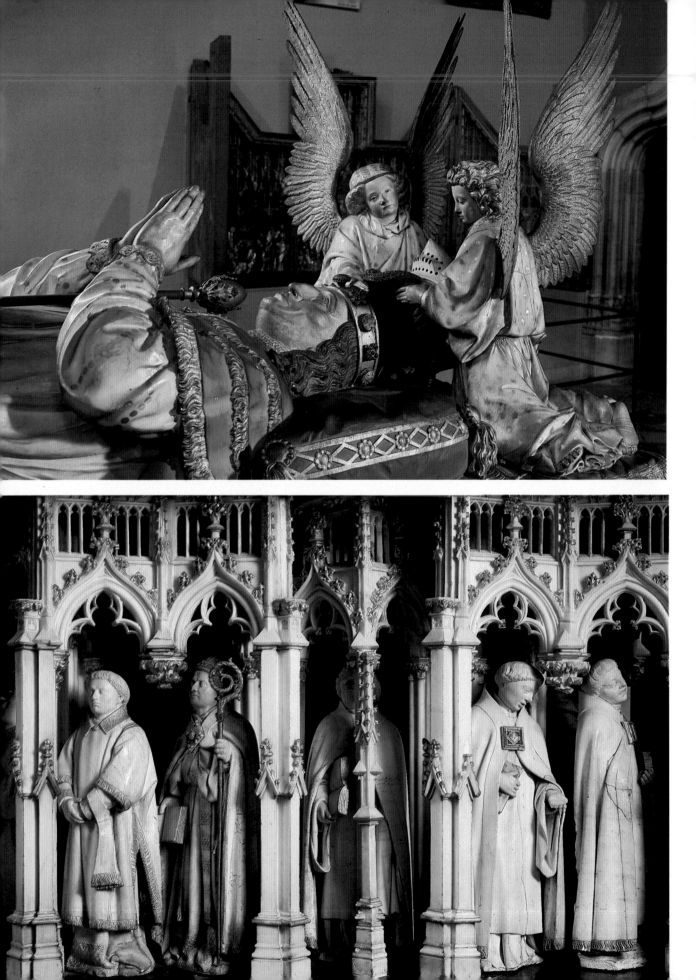

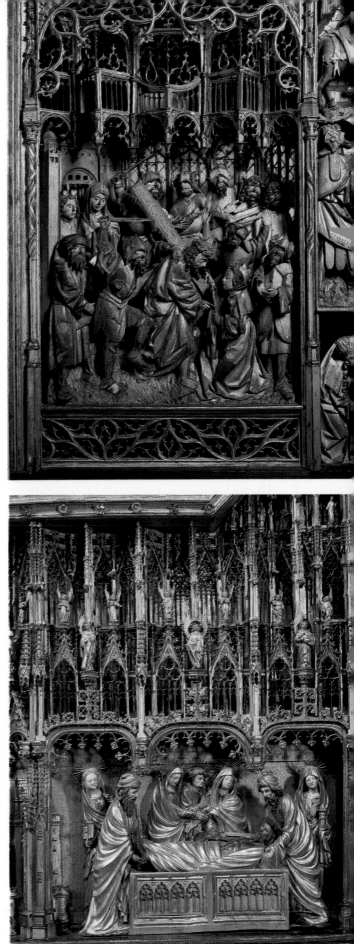

(Above) Detail of the weeping figures. The other two reliefs depict the Passion and the "Mise au Tombeau" by Jacques de Baerze.

(Above left) Philip the Hardy, the founder; (below) a procession of "pleurants" joining in the family's sorrow.

Hardy followed by John the Fearless and Margaret of Bavaria in their wait for the Final Days. The processions for Philip the Good and Isabel of Portugal were probably starting to take shape when the «great collapse of the House of Burgundy» occurred. Duke Charles and Mary, the Emperor Charles V who had desired it so much, never joined them...

A speculator, who later became a delegate with evolved ideas who Napoleon sent to the Pantheon, ruined everything during the Revolution. The dispersion was so total that not even at Dijon is it possible to see everything together: Sluter's *Head of Christ*, for example, is in the Archaeological Museum. But what does remain, collected here by the town's confused compassion, can still marvel. And also sadden...

48

Along the Streets of Old Dijon

Now you hold all the keys to the town. We should not only retain the key of nostalgia. The sentiment expressed by Fernand Gregh makes it easy to scour the past:

> *«..débris d'un passé triomphal*
> *beaté dont on s'énivre et chagrin qui fait mal.»*

There are no more dukes or alcades, wax-warming councillors, or master-spurmakers, the canons are dressed in shadows and even the joyful ladies of the vapour baths seemed to have disappeared... We have to resign ourselves to this. Paul Fort put this resolution in the heart of the adventurers of open sea fishing, times were no longer the same for them either:

> *«Maintenant il y a la République*
> *Et il y a le Président!*
> *Mais il y a plus de baleines!»*

See this little tower – it has a story behind it which is not at all sad... It is situated next to the **Berbis Palace**, the XVIIIth century residence of a noble magistrate. This shrewd, rather surly jurist was married to a beautiful young school girl. The young lady was bored living in that house... One evening, whilst a young officer entertained her with pleasant conversation, the old man came home earlier than expected from his lands. The innocent «tête-

(Above left) Place des Ducs: an old house and the Berbis Palace. (Below) rue Verrerie and rue du Bourg.

Two views of the Vogüé Palace.

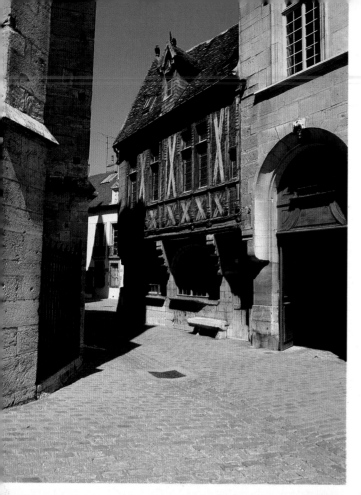

à-tête» could have been misunderstood, so a maid-servant pushed the soldier into the tower, quickly handing him his sword and clothes. He jumped... the lady's honour was saved, but not her sweetheart's leg, which was broken in the fall. Thus, when the King's lieutenants passed by, there was always one who said, in a dreamy voice: «The Presidentess of Berbis was very beautiful, but the tower was too high...»

All around *Notre-Dame du Marché* a tangle of pedestrian streets will randomly lead you onwards. Try not to lose sight of the bell-tower. You will discover the trade and craftwork quarter of the Middle Ages with one peculiarity: the **Vogue Palace**, built by a powerful parliamentary family at the beginning of the XVIIth century. The roof is made of painted tiles: we are in Burgundy; the Renaissance courtyard is a jewel of pink marble: a dream of Italy...

The **Church of Notre-Dame**, built in the XIIIth century, was the parish church of the middle-classes, who were very proud of it: in 1814, the mayor wished to honour it by offering holy water to the Emperor of Austria, not realizing that his gesture shocked... Since the community was only able to afford to buy a rather small piece of land, the architect was obliged to think up some bold technical solutions, the first one being the huge façade «blocking» the thrusts of the nave which is relieved by small pillars and decorated with *gargoyles*. It seems that one day one of these figures fell on top of a young bride after the wedding ceremony. Nobody has ever been able to dis-

(Left) Rue de la Chouette; (below) the church of Notre-Dame: the façade with the gargoyles and apse.

Hôtel Chambellan, rue des Forges: (above) the keystone of the staircase, (right) a complete view of the tower.

cover the date of this very symbolic episode, but that does not change the fact that the inhabitants of Dijon, myself included, blindly believe in the story. In the tower, the «*Jacquemart*», with a pipe in his mouth, strikes the hours. When he came to Dijon from Flanders, stolen from the Tower of *Courtrai* by Duke Philip on the eve of the victory of *Westrosebeke* (1382), he was alone. Dijon gave him a family. They owed it to him! Before he arrived the town lived according to the rhythms of the seasons which are those «of the birds in the sky and the lilies in the fields...». The «*Jacquemart*» substituted the changeable pealing of convent bells with *lay hours*, which never changed from season to season, by day or by night. This was Burgundy's first *clock*.

Our Lady of Good Hope is worshipped here, with the touching image of an XIth century «Black Vergin». It is certain that she saved Dijon from the Swiss in 1513: the beautiful votive tapestry is kept in the museum's «Guards' Hall». Her intervention during the Second World War is not so certain: *Canon Kir*, who was mayor of Dijon although he confessed at Notre-Dame, claimed – not without reason – that it was not of small account... The *stained glass windows* are interesting. If you hear the organ playing, remember for a moment that it was once played by *Jean-Philippe Rameau...*

Another couple of things: in *rue de la Chouette (Owl Street)*, to the left of the church, do not forget to touch the sculpture of the bird of wisdom, symbol of the builder-

The Liégeard Palace.

The Palace of the Parliament of Burgundy.

confrères, which is now polished thanks to the familiar gesture by which a true inhabitant of Dijon can be identified; in *rue de la Forge (Forge Street)* you can enter the courtyard of the **Hôtel Chambellan**: the keystone of the XVth century staircase is an admirable invention, not lacking in humour since the whole weight of the magnificence of this rich man's house is entrusted to a vine-dresser...

Dignity reigns in the quarter where the **Law Courts** are situated – to the south of the Place d'Armes.

The supreme courts still hold their sessions in Burgundy's ancient *Parliament*. However, this will not mean thay you cannot enter: the tax collectors, municipal clerks and officials shut themselves inside, but the magistrates officiate in public. A trial held behind closed doors, for no special reason, could be declared invalid... The *Hall of Lost Passages* has a marvellous elevation. Imagine the spectacle on the day of the solemn reopening when three bishops prepared to celebrate the *Red Mass* in the Chapel of the Holy Spirit. A crowd of solicitors, registrars and lawyers would gather in the nave. Noble chevaliers with their swords unsheathed preceded the eight presidents of Parliament, the sixty-four lay councillors and the five clerical councillors. Only the mitred abbot of Citeaux could lead the formidable «Monsieur le Premier» to his place. On normal days, more informally, the hall was animated by an elegant company: lawyers solicitors, notaries and book-sellers. The young councillors – who enjoyed showing themselves off at the Jeu de Paume «in bold garments» – displayed serious behaviour in the honour of some fascinating people who claimed to know Hebrew...

The fact is that the class of *men in red* was dangerously erudite. In the buildings whose halls were covered with massive folios with gilded and fawn-coloured spines, collections bound in worked or marbled calfskin with the titles in red and manuscripts covered in black velvet or white parchment, animated refectories were formed. People wondered whether the Academy of Dijon had done well to recognize the anonymous memoirs regarding the *purge of customs* written by an unknown young man of Geneva: *Jean-Jacques Rousseau.* If only the powerful magistrates had known what type of purge the disciples of this gentle reformer would reserve them... Sometimes concerts were held in the decorated galleries. One evening, everyone was invited by Mgr the Prince of Condé to listen to *Mozart*: the child prodigy entertained them... It is not certain whether all of this was very merry.

The lower people of the buildings and others of humbler origins amused themselves with the masked parades of the *Compagnie de la Mère Folle*, acting out the satirical stanzas in the dialect of *La Monnaye*, and getting great pleasure out of bad epigram writers, such as that certain Piron who wrote his own epitaph: «He was nobody, not even an academic». A new type of youth was coming out of the colleges, which believed it was able to invent a new world. In 1789 it tried to do just that...

The most famous of these colleges was the one run by the *Jesuits*. Its Chapel is today the reading room of the **Municipal Library**. Many treasures have been gathered there, including the Citeaux manuscripts illuminated during Saint Etienne Harding's time. It is a shame that you cannot spend more time there. The spirit of parliamentary Dijon reigns, the lover of beautiful books. The whole quarter is soaked in this spirit: you will find yourself pausing to look at *book-shops selling ancient volumes* and *book-binders*. Maybe you will find a copy of this work by Eugène Fyot: *Dijon, son passé évoqué par ses rues (Dijon's past evoked by its streets)*, which remains the most spiritual guide-book.

LE BAREUZAI

A naked young man laughs in the middle of a rather serious square. At last a gesture to remind us that Dijon was once a happy winemakers' town! For at least fifteen centuries the *hills of Dijon* were the pride and joy of the Burgundy of frank and fullbodied wines. When the experts declared that the grapes were ripe, the «viscount-major» rode on horseback along the wine tracks – from *Marcs d'Or* to *Violette* – proclaiming the beginning of the *harvest*. A crowd of labourers, recruited in the square of the church of Saint-Philibert, walked up towards the vineyards belonging to dukes, kings and the Gentlemen of Parliament... The wine «trades» – coopers, middlemen, «sworn tasters» – were all hard at work and the «town houses» of the Orders were all turned into cellars, like the *Cellier de Clairvaux* which has been preserved.

Two views of Place François Rude.

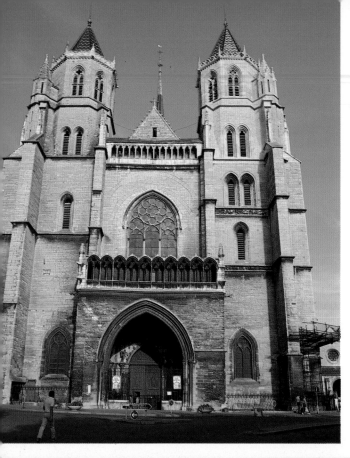

The abbey of Saint-Bénigne, a cathedral since 1792. (Below) the crypt of the Saints and Martyrs.

Le Bareuzai – the vine-dresser of the old songs intoned whilst treading grapes – dances in the very heart of the town. Luckily, he is not alone: the market is nearby; the concerts held at the end of Spring gather together young enthusiasts; the first Sunday of September the *Festival of the Vine* sees him surrounded by the happy processions of the most spontaneous folkloristic festival in Europe. In the nearby trading streets you will find beautiful presentations of wine and all the specialities of Dijon: *cassis (black-currant), wild plum liqueurs, mustard, pain d'épices (ginger-bread)*. I even know a trader who sells *pêches de vigne*, those peaches which ripen with the grapes and which go with the powdery hybrids ripened in refrigerator lorries like a *Corton-Charlemagne* goes with Coca-Cola.

The origins

It seems that Dijon once had «a hundred bell-towers». The image is correct. The people of Dijon were derisive and very religious. They were hard workers. Then, in order to give some meaning to their lives, they joked and prayed to a loud accompaniment of bells. «*In Dijon,* wrote Paradin in the XVIth century, *they meditate like they ring their bells...*». Think of Dijon's churches as places for meeting and celebrating.

Saint-Bénigne is an extraordinarily old sanctuary. Back in the VIth century a monastery was founded to house the relics of the Apostle of Burgundy. It was sacred land. For Christians it was a blessing to be laid to rest there. The crypts contain martyrs and witnesses: the abbot beheaded by the Normans and the mother of Saint Bernard; the church holds princes and rich men: their proximity to the altar is in proportion to their fear of the Final Judgement; the humble people are outside: their tombs amassed together like an army. Nowadays some religious people turn up their noses: according to them «Saint Bénigne» is not sufficiently well known. The large crowd on Resurrection Day will contradict their scruples... The abbey has been continually rebuilt. It has been Merovingian, Carlovingian, Romanesque and Gothic. Around about the year one thousand, a monk of Saint Bénigne, *Raoul Glaber*, wrote: «*The world rejects, it shakes off old age in order to reclothe everywhere with the white ornament of the churches*». He met the Devil at Saint-Léger de Champeaux who presented him with an interesting programme enslaving souls to pride, violence and money... When the dukes first entered the town, the community greeted them in the *Galerie du Gloria*, above the great vestibule. Then at the «altar of Mgr Saint-Bénigne», the duke – take note because he was often an important person, like *Philip the Good* who ruled over half of Europe – swore to «respect the liberty and privileges of Burgundy». The «viscount-major», standing up, placed a venerable ring on his finger, putting a seal to a freely agreed upon alliance. During the Revolution this *symbolic ring* was stolen and was never found again...

The XIVth century abbatial church – now a cathedral – was erected on the site of a *Romanesque crypt*. It is essential to make a pilgrimage to the Apostle's Sarcophagus and listen to the lesson of silence in the forest of pillars of the rotunda. In the *Benedictine Dormitory*, to the north, the **Archaeological Museum** will confront you with a time in which every question was a source of anguish. At the *Origins of the Seine*, the Romanized Celts offered pathetic votive gifts of wood and stone to the goddess *Sequana*: the faces of blind children, tortured women, men who are nothing but sorrow. How much hope was needed by the world in those times!

Saint-Philibert, situated close by, was the parish church of the vine-dressers. It is a XIIth century jewel. Every year, the «louée» – the hiring of labourers for the harvest – was celebrated here, and from time to time there was the joy of a healthy rebellion.

Saint-Michel, to the east of the Palace quarter, is a unique example of the transition from flamboyant Gothic to Renaissance style. The *Sacred Host* was worshipped here, offered by a Pope to a duke who had fought around Mount Thabor.

(Above) The church of Saint-Michel; (below) the church of Saint-Philibert.

The past rediscovered

Long before the big movement of interest in «popular arts and traditions», the systematization of the «ecomuseum» concept, the passion for folk songs and the discovery of «fest noz» by the ultra left, a learned Burgundian, Maurice Perrin de Puycousin (1856-1949), compiled collections of *testimonies* regarding rural civilization. It was about time: the way of life which was a *way of being* would soon be cancelled out by two World Wars.

The collections are held at Tournus and Dijon. At Dijon they make up the nucleus of an admirable **Museum of Burgundian Life**, an example of incredible imagination. Permanent exhibitions and temporary shows converse in Rue Sainte-Anne with subtle counterpoint. Nearby, the **Museum of Sacred Art** displays anonymous masterpieces from humble village churches.

Images of the past: from printing to photography.

(Right) Interiors of XIXth century southern Burgundy.

The memory of the stones

The XIXth century town planning of Dijon has only one merit: the absence of complexes. Entire quarters, sometimes of vast dimensions, have been constructed with great constancy of banality. Without forgetting the witnesses which have disappeared – *Louis XI's Gendarmes' Castle* replaced by a «kitsch» Post Office – and the spaces utilized in such a mediocre way – *the ramparts of Porte Guillaume* – it still has an antiquated charm. However, we cannot forgive the example of contempt for its medieval past which it has given to the rest of Burgundy. A lack of culture – which should never be understimated – and a spirit of profit-making – the sale of the *Holy Chapel's* stained glass windows to the «Victoria and Albert Museum» must have earned somebody something... – are not the only guilty parties. There was also a «hatred of priests», which was doubtless a determining factor in the sackings which continued well beyond the revolutionary period. At the **Carthusian monastery of Champmol**, what remains of *Sluter's* works: the base of the «Calvary of the Prophets», and the «Portal of the Chapel», stirs up emotions of compassion and anger. **Citeaux** – that privileged place (see Fontenay) – was razed to the ground and the ashes of the first generation Dukes thrown to the wind like those of the Dukes of Valois. At least the Cistercians rebuilt their community. The chapel is open to all for the six offices and two daily masses.

(Above left) Place Darcy and "Porte Guillaume"; (below) the Bear by François Pompon in the Darcy garden.

(Right) The base of the Prophets in Sluter's "Calvary"; (below) Citeaux, the ancient library (XIIIth century).

THE COTE-D'OR

One day, a brilliant businessman, who was not a Burgundian, travelled along the Côte, from *Chenôve*, where the XIIth century presses of the Capetian dukes are preserved, to *Santenay*. What he admired most, along these 54 enchanted kilometres, was the region's talent for public relations: «You have managed to call all your villages after great wines...».

Semi-naïvety: several communes have added the name of their most famous wine to their traditional one. From the north to the south, from the generous reds to the sublime whites – with excellent points for reds and whites – the triomphal procession winds along from the *Côte de Nuits* to the *Côte de Beaune*: Fixin, Gevrey-*Chambertin*, Morey-*Saint Denis*, Chambolle-*Musigny*, Vougeot, Flagey-*Echezeaux*, Vosne-*Romanée*, Nuits-*Saint-Georges*, Premeaux-Prissey, Pernand-*Vergelesses*, Aloxe-*Corton*, Savigny, Chorey, Beaune, Pommard, Volnay, Monthelie,

Auxey-*Duresses*, Meursault, Saint-Aubin, Puligny and Chassagne-*Montrachet*, Santenay.

The Côte – which does not represent the whole of Burgundy's winemaking areas, but is its heart and its model – is the slope of the «very dry and very ugly hill» that Stendhal saw. It gave its name to the department created by the Revolution within the old duchy. Its gold autumn cloak seduced the Committees who, luckily, gave up the idea of the proposed aquatic name of «Seine et Saône»... The *Hautes-Côtes*, won back after half a century around picturesque villages, make up the hinterland. The vineyards do not venture onto the plains, beyond the limestone dominated soils. Man's wisdom has relegated them amongst the stones. The Mediterranean liana needs rigid surveillance, it has to be supervised in the deep and heavy soils with water, fertilizers and various improvements. If left to the folly of its growth, it branches out and

FROM THE VINE TO THE GLASS

The wines of Burgundy in general, and those of the Côte d'Or in particular, have been the subject of many studies. When setting up a vicitultural library, the same rules used in the cellar should be applied: it is better to buy from the viticulturist than from the supermarket. Advice on the art of appreciating wine flourishes from the pens of – or is signed by... – polygraphic cooks, heavy sociologists and fashionable ladies. But the advisers are not the ones who do the drinking... From the vine to the glass many things can happen – some of which are subtle and elusive – which only the true Burgundian sensitivity can appreciate. Some of the best works from cellars are available in various languages.

Some «good bottles»:

Camille Rodier	Le vin de Bourgogne
René Engel	Propos sur l'art de bien boire
Pierre Poupon	Nouvelles pensées d'un dégustateur

A good «cellar stock»:

| Charles Quittanson | Connaissance et gloire du vin |

«Daytime companions»:

| Jean-François Bazin | La Côte, village par village *(a notable collection of monographs)* |

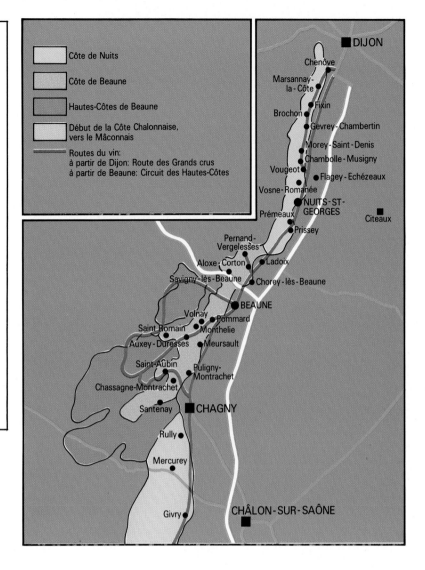

Côte de Nuits

Côte de Beaune

Hautes-Côtes de Beaune

Début de la Côte Chalonnaise, vers le Mâconnais

Routes du vin:
à partir de Dijon: Route des Grands crus
à partir de Beaune: Circuit des Hautes-Côtes

expands, shading its own fruits and causing the sun to ripen them unevenly, thus producing horrors...; on the stony slopes, the long roots search for life amongst the secrets of the earth and, with the rare sap, nourish stocks which, when rigorously pruned and weeded, do not generate wood or leaves, but heavy bunches of grapes which, in the autumn, burst with sugar and vibrate with aroma. Great wines come from the mystical practices of the vines.

Every human work is exposed to the risks of history. A miracle of collective will made it possible to respect – for two thousand years – the demand for quality, in the face of the jealousy of Rome, who had *Domitian* give the order to uproot the vineyards of Beaune and Nuits and introduced revenue – a pitiful destructor – in order to attack their lucky competitor. In the XIVth century, the Court of the Popes of Avignon had the selected wines sent, in new casks, on boats along the Saône. They sought after these wines so much that finally *Petrarch* accused the cardinals

of preventing the Pontiff from returning to Rome «for fear of being deprived of the wine of Beaune...». The Dukes of Burgundy, «lords of the best wines in Christendom», issued a Grand Decree in 1396 establishing all the principles subsequently maintained by the King's cultural authorities, from the chapters of the cathedrals, to the regular orders and from the «Messieurs du Parlement» up to the Revolution. Despite the parcelling off of large properties, the *phylloxera* which killed off the stocks and the wars which sacrified the young men; despite the enemies of today: easy money, disastrous credits; a stupid tax which hits workers, the «preservation» and the successions; the power of distribution and technocracy.

Despite all of this Burgundy holds firmly onto its course. In the *tastevin* – the silver cupping-glass with chiselled reliefs for distinguishing the «colour» on one side and the «body» on the other – sixty generations of winemakers invite you to the festivities.

FIXIN

A typical village which has remained intact: the *church* with its bell-tower covered in coloured tiles, the *feudal oven* covered in lavic stones, the *wash-house*. The distribution of cultivations which remains unchanged as far as the hills of the Saône and the Loire, to the south, is clearly visible: the cereal-growing plains, the hills of vineyards and the slightly wooded and uncultivated «mountain». All of this enjoys excellent exposure to the sun. The wine of *Perrière*, an ancient Cistercian property, merits complete respect.

A captain of the Imperial Guard, Claude Noisot, built a place of Napoleonic recollections here. The memory itself inspired the form. Bonaparte's lieutenant was garrisoned at *Auxonne* in the Côte d'Or for Louis XVI, and was one of the first to disperse the revolutionary-apprentices of the Val-de-Saône. Of all the soldiers that Burgundy gave him: Davout, Junot, Marmont... the most loyal and most touching soldier was Noisot, who followed the emperor to Saint Helena. The cottage-museum dedicated to vanished glories, the «hundred step» staircase – in memory of the the One Hundred Days – the tomb itself of the grenadier are all very touching. But Noisot had a friend: François Rude, the son of the blacksmith in Rue du Lacet at Dijon, creator of the *Marseillaise* of the «Arc de Triomphe» at the «Etoile» in Paris, who realized his second masterpiece for Noisot: *Napoleon awakening to Immortality.* This is a powerful work of art. It is ideally surrounded by the background of light and shadow created by the large trees.

(Left) Napoleon awakening to Immortality, by François Rude. (Below) a view of the town.

(Right) Two views of Gevrey-Chambertin.

GEVREY-CHAMBERTIN

Napoleon again! The emperor particularly appreciated the wines of this village. The heavy travelling carriage – seen from Hamburg to Moscow and from Madrid to Vienna – transported an entire cellar and in the evenings the simpleton Roustan pulled out bottles of *Chambertin*. An ugly legend claims that water was mixed with the wine! I remember the disbelief with which we greeted this sacrilegious story at school... The sovereign of red wines for this first part of the Côte de Nuits is produced exclusively in the 13 hectares of the old «champ du Bertin». But the imperial wine enjoys an illustrious escort: *Clos de Bèze, Lastricières, Mazoyères, Charmes, Mazis, Griotte, Chapelle, Ruchottes...* The village has a total of 400 hectares of top quality wine.

If you are only passing by, visit the wine cellars. If you are stopping off, the *Rotisserie du Chambertin* is a must: the smiling host is also a winemaker and an excellent cook; the setting is an ancient house protected by old vaults. If you are staying here, there are many hotels to choose from. Brochon can be easily reached across the *Castle* vineyards; the first *Hautes-Côtes* can be discovered across the *coombe of Lavaux*. The warm memory of *Gaston Roupnel* (1872-1946) can be found in the Place des Marronniers in the village centre, where he lived. He was the first historian of the French countryside, the novelist of the people of the vineyards and wines, the immortal originator of a delicious recipe for «potée» (a typical dish based on boiled meat and vegetables, often using pork).

The castle of Brochon.

*(Above right) The "Clos de Vougeot", temple of Burgundy.
(Below) the country castle (XVIth century).*

BROCHON

A word about the itineraries of the land of wine. Ge-vrey-Chambertin – which not long ago could be reached by an electric tramway which dragged the open trailers across the vines – is the meeting point of many roads. Avoid the main road crossing the plain. Half way up the hill, the *wine road* will take you from village to village. Beyond the ridge, from coombe to coombe, there is the road of the *Hautes-Côtes*. If you want to walk, the *vineyard paths* will enable you to pass from one commune to another. Discovering these paths is a joy. According to the rhythm of the seasonal labours, you will meet vinegrowers working with all of their special tools: the *enjambeurs* – tractors constructed in Burgundy for their vineyards which transport the various implements by advancing «on horseback» along the rows of vines. You might see helicopters in a mist of antiparasite products, but above all you will meet men and women bent over the vines, from pruning through to harvest time.

Brochon should be approached through the vines. It is a pleasant village with a surprising **castle**. This was the work of a poet, *Stephen Liégeard* who, at the end of the last century, won the «Jeux Floraux de Toulouse» and was the model for *Alphonse Daudet's* «country subprefect». He had a «pastiche» of the castles of the Loire built and invented the happy name of «Côte d'Azur» for the French Riviera. The inopportune presence of the Ministry of Education should not prevent you from evoking that nightingale which asked: «Is a subprefect bad?»...

THE «CLOS» OF VOUGEOT

Saint Bernard described some monks who were too attached to the «*tastevin*»: «Three or four times during the same meal a half-full cupping-glass is brought along: it is sniffed more than drunk, tasted more than drunk, and finally, with sure taste and rapid decision, the best wine of all is chosen...» The sons of Citeaux bought some uncultivated land at *Vougeot*, for the price of two fustian tunics. They planted a vine there and bordered it with a wall, as had been established by Burgundian law since the VIth century. Great care was taken of their «clos»: the Order, which had been wisely informed, indicated the use of soft water; the *Scriptures* were happy about the attention the Master gave to stocks, presses and vine-dressers; Bernard himself meditated on the text of the «Song of Solomon»:

> «*Catch the foxes,
> the foxes who destroy the vines,
> because our vines are in flower...*»

From the XIIth to the XVth century, the borders of the «clos» were fixed at 50 hectares. Eighty-four owners have now divided it into 200.000 bottles. The XVIth century *Castle*, the XIIth century *cellar*, the *fermentation rooms* with their huge medieval presses, are today the head-quarters of the «*Chevaliers du Tastevin*». We will meet up with them again. To be invited to their table is a feast, their company is a privilege and to visit their head-quarters is «one of the important moments» of the Burgundian itinerary.

Beaune, at the foot of the Côte, on the edges of the forest...

BEAUNE

The foundations of Burgundy are here, in Beaune; a town of 20.000 inhabitants whose economic power greatly surpasses its appearance of an average town.

Beaune was born from... a spring of fresh water. The Celtic horsemen, with their long iron swords, who came from the East five centuries B.C., loved only joyful people. The priests of *Benelos*, the spirit of spring-waters, gathered at the foot of the hill around the place from which the waters flowed, and laughed with joy. The pilgrimage site – *Belena* – became a market-place: *Beaune*. Stones were heaped together to protect it: a *murus gallicus* of logs and rocks, a complex device from the Roman *castrum*, and the remains of pagan temples were used for the walls raised against the barbarians. You can cover this part of the history at the *«Soleil» (Sun) Motorway Archeodrome*, which has had an enormous success, because the scientific rigour has remained discreet, allowing the magic of the dark ages to take over its halls.

Then there was the *Duke's peace*. The census of names tells of the birth of a people of workers within the town and its seven suburbs. The cunning or naïvety of the neighbours often inspired nicknames which, taking their cue from physical or other features, led to the creation of names such as: the Handsome One, the Ugly One, the Lame One, Big Eyes, the Well-Adorned One; there were some more fanciful names, too: Robin the Sword,

Symonot the Good Heart, Jehan of the vines and Jehan of the skies... I wonder if the two young people, listed in the duke's census as Handsome Jehan and the Pretty One, ever met? Soon, trade names began to appear amongst the more powerful nicknames: Vine-dresser, Cooper, Carpenter, Woollen-Draper... Medieval Beaune led a happy life: the wine, of course, but also the cloths contributed to create great animation. It was also, with its *Parliament*, the judicial capital of the duchy.

Beaune had great difficulty in accepting royal power. In 1478, *Philippe de Chaumergy* headed a rebellion which led the town to recognize the authority of John IV of Châlon, Prince of Orange, «lieutenant of Madame the Duchess of Austria and this part of Burgundy». Louis XI got his revenge by transferring the Parliament from Beaune to Dijon. Many people visited Beaune, however, attracted by its fame of antiquity, compassion and wealth. Queen *Christine of Sweden* was greeted by the sound of a singular band: «four drums, then three drums, then one drum, then another drum and, finally, the two drums of Nolay brought in as reinforcements...» At Carmel, *Louis XIV* and his mother, *Anne of Austria*, wished to thank the community whose prayers had brought to the kingdom the – tardy... – joy of the birth of the Sun King. The smuggler, *Mandrin*, blackmailed the revenue authorities. They nourished rancour for the mayor who had six of the best bottles from his cellar brought up to drink with the brigand while they waited for the money to be counted. Mandrin only stole from the State. The common people admired him and sang:

«Compagnons de misère
Allez dire à ma mère
Qu'elle ne m'reverra plus
J'suis un enfant perdu...»

The town's imagination did not subside with time. *Gaspard Monge* (1746-1818), together with the son of the notary of Nolay, Lazare Carnot, armed revolutionary France against invasion and founded the Polytechnic School. *Jules-Etienne Marey* (1853-1904), a physiologist, used photography to help study living functions. We owe to this man's research that other plastic space which is one of the XXth century's main resources, medical monitoring and the cinema... *Paul Masson* (1859-1940), following in the footsteps of the cooper, Parent, who persuaded *Jefferson* that French wines had a place at the White House, conquered a winemaking empire... in California. At the **Civic Museum**, some original collections make it possible to relive, amongst others, these pages of modern history which tell of times that were certainly very productive.

The Prince-President directed the railway towards Dijon. The capital of Burgundy grew, accumulating factories, eating up its vineyards, following chimeras... Beaune decided to devote itself to wine. This was not always easy although, naturally, Beaune had the right qualifications for the job, first of all the quality of its soil: over 500 hectares, divided up into sixty «climats» with evocative names: *Bressandes, Clos de Mouches* – the bees of Burgundy – *Marconnets...* which one has to know how to interpret. A Prime Minister of the Vth Republic was very surprised to see a 1968 «*La Montée Rouge*» (red ascent) served, followed by a «*Grèves*» (meaning both «strike» and «shore» in French)... The denominations only evoke the Oxford type marl which appears at the sides of an ancient pathway and the dry and slightly sandy soil of one side of Mount Battois. Relations with the Côte went back a long time, but the villagers wanted to keep their own identity: thus *Savigny* and *Pommard* have their own *Cousinerie* and their own *Baillage*, with a justly shady brotherhood, and try telling *Meursault* and *Nuits* that they are «dependant» on Beaune! It was, therefore, necessary to propose a service and not impose a domination. Only a remarkable commercial ability made it possible to face the gamble: thanks to its own marketing experience, Beaune guided the smaller owners; the big wineries inherited from monastic orders made it possible to create the wine; family-run enterprises were helped to absorb the shock of bad vintages, break-downs in sales and increases in credit rates. You can visit Beaune's wineries. They are mostly true and proper monuments covering several levels, kept at different temperatures. Thousands of professional people – from the teacher at the *viticultural Lycée* to the printer – live with the vine, just like the vinegrower, at the mercy of the flowering, the storms and the sun.

This is why Beaune lives with its nose in the air, ready to detect the enemies of winemaking: rain, frost and hail. The **Hôtel-Dieu (Main Hospital)** is crowned by fifty

The square near the "Hôtel-Dieu".

gilded iron weather-vanes.

The duke's chancellor, *Nicolas Rolin*, ruled for forty years: enough to fear God's Judgement. The only people who could intervene in his favour were the poor: Nicolas and his wife, *Guigone de Salins*, decided to build them a place to live. It was intended to be more beautiful than the Princes' Palace, because it was destined for those closest to God, much closer than the King's courtiers.

The model is that of *Hainaut*: the Hospital Saint-Jacques of Valenciennes, with its hospital Ladies and its architect. But the execution of the project is all *Burgundian*: the oak structures, coloured tiles, and design of the windows and roofs. Most importantly, the Hôtel-Dieu leans against the town walls, and is built over huge cellars, near the main vat-rooms: it is well-rooted in the soil of Beaune, born from its land, from its «climats», inseparable from the vine – the source of all nourishment. The hospital has been standing intact, marvellous and loyal since 1443. On the third Sunday of November, the courtyard is covered in Flanders tapestries. In the medieval entrance hall, the *Charitable Institutions of Beaune* sell the year's vintage of their properties by candle auction: 58 hectares of the best wines. The proceeds go to the modernization of the Hospital. It is the biggest charity auction in the world.

Whilst a cheerful chime plays the notes of old songs telling of hope and love, under the fists of the «*trézeleur*», in the spire, you can enter the house of the poor.

Join the 400.000 visitors who each year try to understand the *soul* of this place. Leave behind «modern»

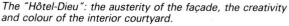

The "Hôtel-Dieu": the austerity of the façade, the creativity and colour of the interior courtyard.

prejudices: no, death is not a conclusion, the moment of which can be postponed by buying health and which should be hidden as a scandal or a failure; no, beauty is not a luxury reserved for the wealthy, the aesthetes and the museums, to be left out of the everyday life of everyone else. The Hôtel-Dieu of Beaune is a *place of transit*. The *Christ de Pitié*, sublime figure of the XVth century, dominates the main hall (Grande Salle). He took on the burden, once and for all, of all human suffering. His sorrowful expression watches over these vessels of pain sailing towards Eternity. This is a *place of perfection*. Observe every single object: the coverlets, the pewter pitchers, the pottery in the pharmacy. The floor itself, covered in tiles decorated with images, the sparkling copper, and the automated rotisserie in the kitchen all contribute to the harmony of this work of art.

The retablo of the *Last Judgement* was kept in the Main Hall, above the altar. Do not crowd together with the naïve holding a magnifying glass to see «the wild strawberries» of Paradise. *Roger van der Weyden* – the mysterious painter of Tournai – painted a drama not an anecdote. At the moment of the final agony, the doors were opened onto the Archangel and the Supreme Judge. The last thing the dying person saw was *an immense light...*

Ever since the Middle Ages, Beaune has engraved the image of the Virgin Mother on its seal and arms. In her hands she holds a bunch of grapes and is surrounded by the motto: *causa nostra laetitia*, the source of our joy. In the century of the sceptics, the echevins feared that those of bad faith – from Dijon in particular – would attribute

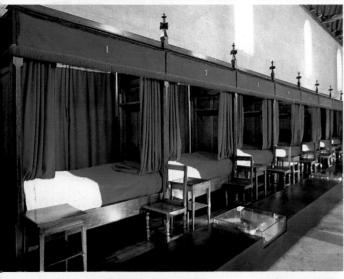

The four photographs on this page show us a general view of the Main Hall of the Hôtel-Dieu, the beds for the sick, a view of the ancient pharmacy and a display case containing the pewter objects used in the 15th century by the patients.

On the right: patient care, in a scenic reconstruction in the sacristy; a minutely-detailed reconstruction of the ancient kitchens.

*Below: the Last Judgment by Roger van der Weyden.
The altarpiece was commissioned to the artist from Tournai in 1443 expressly for the Hôtel-Dieu, where it is still preserved.*

Church of Notre-Dame.

(Right) Tapestries telling the Life of Mary.

Beaune's joy to the bunch of grapes rather than to Our Lady, and substituted the sentence with: *urbis et orbis honnos*, «honour» in its meaning of sovereignty and officialism, of the town and of the world.

The **Church of Notre-Dame**, more than the *Tower* of Philip the Hardy, dominates Beaune. The pride and heart of the town, the«Illustrious Collegiate Church», recently raised to the rank of basilica, has been constantly altered and embellished since 1120. Today the Romanesque and Gothic elements give it strength and elegance. The huge vestibule, the narthex and the high nave are an admirable example of creativity and balance. The chapter *cloister* is a marvel of light. The *tapestries telling Mary's story* were weaved in Flanders based on cartoons by the Burgundian, Pierre Spicre, and were commissioned by Cardinal Rolin, the chancellor's brother. We are in the autumn of the Middle Ages, when the glory of the Great Dukes of the West blazed. Since the outline of Italy was being formed, the Renaissance, too, was not a rupture but an evolution... Since 1500, the *tapestries of Notre-Dame* have told the Holy Story: a thousand flowers illuminate the landscapes, the saints are dressed in gold brocade and the shepherds, kneeling down amidst white sheep, listen to the words of the smiling angels...

Think of Notre-Dame as the parish church of Beaune. The town was often shaken by riots, especially on the occasion of the local elections, which have always been greatly contended. In 1452, Beaune actually had two mayors. They both claimed to have won the election and offered bread and cherries to their devotees. The duke had to organize a nice ceremony of reconciliation at Notre-Dame: the rebellion of Gand was nothing in comparison... The *Confraternity of the Arquebus*, during the reign of Louis XV, used to meet at the foot of the altar, with its members dressed in scarlet red with yellow silk revers. Cardinal Roncalli, who later became *Pope John XXIII*, prayed here. It is definitely not an ordinary church...

Of course, you are visiting Beaune by foot. This is the only way to visit the town. You can leave your car on the surrounding avenues at the foot of the walls which Louis XI made the people of Beaune pay for in order to atone for their spirit of independence: but the town got its revenge by transforming the **ramparts** and the King's barracks into cellars... The heart of the town is not very large, but it is quite unpredictable. The churches: **Notre-Dame**, the superb **Saint-Nicolas** on the outskirts of the town, the **Chapelle du Temple** where the last great master of the «Poor Knights of Christ» Jacques de Molay, who was burned to death by Philip the Handsome, took his vows, have prepared you for a medieval town. The Hotel-

Two views of old houses in the town centre.

Dieu has transported you to the radiant duchy of «Monseigneur de Bourgogne». You will also discover a Renaissance style – elegant and affected – and many classical buildings of the great French eras... Be a bit curious, go into the courtyards, push the doors open, ask to be guided around. The treasures: open-air stairways, unreal balconies, hidden gardens, are just beyond the threshold. Every now and again, winding staircases penetrate the rock: under the stone vaults oak casks and tens of thousands of bottles are laid out.

Before adventuring into the streets of *Paradise* and *Hell*, take a look at the **Museum of Wine**. This is located in the ancient palace of the Dukes of Burgundy. The sovereigns used to stay there during the sessions of the legal division of the Court. They also came to watch over the harvesting of their vineyards: a lot of their spirit has remained in the palace. Imagine in this background of stone and wood, these men, lords of at least half of Europe, who knew that power does not have enjoyment as its aim nor terror as its means... Their house is a pleasant one. A beautiful tapestry by *Lurçat*, woven especially for the palace, decorates the gala hall. The history of the vine and wine is told by what was France's first **ecomuseum**. A collection of *presses* gives an excellent view of the continuity of traditions in winemaking Burgundy.

The most important thing is the vinegrower

Leaving Beaune in a hot-air balloon gives an easy interpretation of the landscape. On the steep mountain slope, as the sun rises dispelling the mists and dangerous early morning frosts of early Spring, you can locate the various «climats». These are *spaces dedicated to wine*: the land, the exposure, the vocation. They all host the same noble vines: *Pinot* and *Chardonnay,* but these vines do not respond to the solicitude of the soil and the seasons in the same way. The vine-grower plays a determining rôle. There are no two *Stradivarius* the same, nor two virtuosi who can obtain exactly the same resonance from the same instrument...

The wine-making profession in Burgundy is organized with a severe discipline unequalled in the rest of the world. The territories have fixed boundaries, the yield is controlled, and the origins are identified in detail. The names, or «appellations», are defined according to a pyramidal order: regional, *Burgundy Hautes-Côtes of Beaune*; municipal, *Saint-Aubin*; first «crus», *Mercurey Clos du Roi*; great «crus», *Richebourg* or *Montrachet*. Each «*ouvrée*» of vineyard (corresponding to 4,35 ares) is rigorously marked. Each *cask of wine*, holding 228 litres, is followed through from birth to maturity. The label on each 75 centilitre *bottle* gives a detailed and dated civil status. In order to avoid falsifications, this sort of «wine passport» is often printed under tight surveillance, like bank-notes and, if that were not enough, it is also numbered!

(Right) The Palace of the Dukes of Burgundy; (below) the Museum of Wine.

Panoramic view of the countryside.

Wine tasting should be festive. Do not feel embarassed by the hierarchies and millesimals. The price, of course, is not a bad guide. Over half the Côte's production is exported. An international market has been established which influences the prices. It integrates the more certain values quite well: the character, vintage and preservation; but it is also sensitive to less decisive factors: scarcity, fashion and passing fame. It does not, however, give enough consideration to another determining element: the personality of the *vinegrower*, «*propriétaire-récoltant*» or the «*dealer*». The best wine is not the most expensive one, but the one that gives the most pleasure.

Every year the **Confraternity of the «Chevaliers du Tastevin»** holds two particularly significant events.

The «*Tastevinage*» is the big test of Burgundy's wines. At the Clos de Vougeot Castle, juries made up of vinegrowers, traders, restauranteurs, and qualified winelovers, sit at round tables – it is necessary to be able to talk and nobody has precedence – where they evaluate, without indulgence, the quality of the wines. The bottles are presented wrapped in sheets of paper, with no details given except for a number which refers to the name and the vintage. The wines are not classified in an absurd «Hit-parade», but their qualities are appreciated. The *Meursault-Charmes* wines compete with each other, as do the *Côtes de Beaune Village* wines, according the idea that Burgundy has of how that vintage should be...

The «*Saint-Vincent Tournante*» – at the end of January – honours the men of vines and wines. They walk in procession carrying statues of their patron saint. The Confraternity receives some of the eldest among them. Each year, one of the twenty or twenty-five villages which still follow the tradition of *excellence*, now forgotten elsewhere, becomes the capital of Burgundy for a day.

So set off freely on your voyage of discovery. The vinegrowers are happy to receive any visitors who display more than just plain curiosity and, in many villages, some of the wineries are open to the imagination. At least once in your life you should make contact with a *Romanée-Conti*, a *Corton-Charlemagne* or a *Grand-Echezeaux*. There are, however, some more accessible pleasures. I know an *aligoté* of Pernand – produced from a modest vine, but what a village! – which is well worth the journey... Accompany the wine with *gougères*, light crunchy cheesey pastry, which really excites the palate. At the restaurant, choose the menù first. Avoid any type of affectation: I would not know what to drink with «slices of avocado and clams, accompanied by truffle in raspberry vinegar»... The ancient cuisine of Burgundy is

76

Views of two cellars.

(Right) "La Roche-Pot", fief of a powerful baron of Burgundy.

very varied: eggs in meurette sauce (typical Burgundian sauce based on red wine), best quality ham, fresh-water fish, «coq au vin», game. Do not feel obliged to respect the alleged combinations of wines and dishes. There are some rules of common sense which can be followed: white wines before reds; the range of aromas should increase; cheese is the most harmonious companion of prized wines, salad the worst...

A good Burgundian meal consists of snails cooked in the old-fashioned style accompanied by a *white Beaune wine*, chicken «à la Gaston Gérard» sprinkled with a *Santeny-Gravières* and Chambertin cheese in harmonious dialogue with a great aged *Saint-Georges*, to be appreciated in tranquillity, as though in a dream...

Then you will see how beautiful this land is!

(Left) views of Châlon-sur-Saône; (below right) statue by Nicéphore Niepce.

The old cathredral of Saint-Vincent.

CHALON-SUR-SAONE

First of all there is the river. Through the Rhône, which it flows into at Lyon, the Saône became an important way of penetrating the Mediterranean influences in «middle» Europe. It also made it possible to export northern products to the Roman provinces. For a long time, the Saône was a borderline between the Kingdom and the Empire. A border is at the same time a place of dispute and an occasion for exchange. This past is still very much alive in the small towns of the Côte d'Or, to the north of Châlon: *Auxonne, Saint-Jean de Losne, Seurre*, garrisons and market towns.

The *river* made Châlon's fortune: the price of transporting the casks of wine destined for the Pope from Beaune to the port of Châlon – 27 kilometres by land – cost the same as from Châlon to Avignon – 300 kilometres by river... From the XIIIth century, two *fairs* were held in an immense town of wood and cloth along the banks of the Saône, administrated by an official of the Duke and the «consent of merchants»: the «warm» fair was held in the summer and the «cold» fair at the end of the winter. Two or three hundred draper merchants from Normandy, Brabant, the Empire and Milan made a good trade there. Around them, local traders proposed their furs, ordinary cloths and wines. Free-traders arbitrated

over Savoy currency, Genevan credit and the discounts of the Banks of Lyon. The *leather hide fairs*, much criticized by ecologists, are the last trace of this great medieval market.

The building of a network of *canals* across Burgundy, in the XVIIIth century, gave Châlon a second wind. Today it is a powerful and volitive industrial city. At present, important works are being carried out in a northerly direction: from Marseilles to Rotterdam the imposing *Rhône-Rhine* connection will be open to 5.000 ton towed convoys. The French nuclear power station builders, *Framatome*, already use the river which Roman boats, loaded with amphorae, sailed up two thousand years ago... It is also one of the junctions for river tourism.

The *wines of the Côte of Châlon* are worth mentioning. Some – *Givry, Rully, Mercurey, Montagny, Saint-Véran* – can compete with those of the Côte-d'Or. Discover them at the *Maison des Vins* and in the old quarters of the city centre.

Nicéphore Niepce and *Vivant Denon* are natives of this region. They invented, respectively, photography and Egyptology. Do not forget to visit their museums.

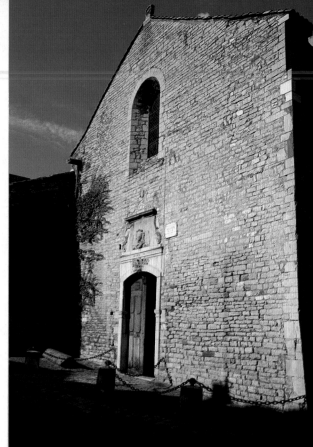

The two towers of the "Porte des Champs", the main entrance in the ancient walls surrounding the abbey.

A church in the old town.

(Right) The abbey of Tournus, the pilgrims' town.

TOURNUS

The harsh winters of Norway give the country's young men a violent desire for adventure and sun, come springtime. Today, their seasonal migration is pacific, but in the VIIIth century it was a source of terror. When their long, agile ships, with a dragon sculptured on the prow, reached the western coasts, the monks ran away, taking their holy relics with them. Burgundy was not spared by the «men from the north, the Normans»: an abbot of Saint-Bénigne of Dijon was beheaded; some churches were burnt down whilst the community, hidden deep in the woods, sang: «*De furor normanorum libera nos, Domine!*»; the monks of Chissey-en-Morvan had to take Saint Anthony to safety... all the way to Brescia! An energetic duke, *Richard the Avenger*, recruited an army and defeated the terrible Scandinavians twice. Burgundy became a refuge. Saint Martin left Tours for *Chablis*, Vivant, Poitiers for *Vergy*; Médard and Silvain, Soisson and Thérouanne for *Dijon*; Flocel and Baudèle, Verdun and Nimes for *Beaune*; Prudent and Florent, Aquitaine for *Bèze* and *Tonnerre*... Burgundy came out wonderfully enriched from the cruel grip of the Vikings: it had become a Holy Land.

In the same way, Saint Philbert came to *Tournus* in 875, together with the monks from the Atlantic island of Noirmoutier. He found Saint Valerian, the old preacher of the region, who refused to hand the crypt over to the new arrival. The construction of the **abbatial church** was begun in the IXth century and was completed in the XIIth century. It is one of the most complex marvels of Romanesque architecture. Its chronology is controversial and there are many influences: from Lombardy to Muslim Spain. But what counts is its power: few sanctuaries in the world impose the gesture of Faith with such authority. The façade is majestic, flanked by two huge towers of the fortified walls; the narthex is sustained by gigantic barbaric pillars and crowned by a subtle play of cross vaults; the nave, with its unforgettable pink light, leads to a secluded choir. The shadows of the *crypt* make it possible to evoke the anguish and hope of the year *One Thousand*; the *abbey buildings* – built between the XIth and XVth century – show the splendour of what was, up until the XVIIth century, one of the most famous independent monastic communities.

The destination of many pilgrimages, the Abbey of Saint Philibert gave life to Tournus. It is pleasant to walk

(Left) The abbatial church of Saint-Philibert; (above) the narthex; (below left) the nave; (below right) the statue of Notre-Dame la Brune.

Costumes from the town of Greuze.

through the town going, for example, down to the river, the Saône, along the streets flanked by old houses. The **Hôtel-Dieu (Main Hospital)** – built during the XVIIth and XVIIIth centuries – illustrates the ancient tradition of hospitality which, in a modern form, has led to the creation of the *Restaurant Greuze*, one of the gastronomic temples of Burgundy. But wherever you go, the superb bell-tower calls you back to the abbey. Once the flow of tourists has dispersed you can come back and meditate. In 1120, Pope Calixte II prayed here. The West plunged into its first «Renaissance», the most decisive one. A solid power guaranteed peace in Burgundy. Arabian *rezzous*, viking raids, bloody Hungarian cavalcades, private gentlemanly wars, were now just nightmares from ancient times. The world appeared to be beautiful and new, under God's gaze.

The serious and serene XIIth century image of *Notre-Dame-la-Brune*, in Auvergne style, has illuminated the warm heart of this ancient town through the centuries.

Jean-Baptiste Greuze (1725-1805) was born in Tournus. A great strength can be perceived beneath his delicate forms of expression. *The Village Sweetheart* (1741, exhibited at the Louvre) well illustrates the dignity of a rural society which deserved other lords than the Marquise of Merteuil and the Chevalier of Valmont... The world of *Fragonard* and that of *David* are separated by a revolution that was not only a pictorial one. The peasants of Greuze, who would not tollerate being scorned, were the actors. In the XIXth century, they still preserved their tradition of quality of the soul and of objects. *Maurice Perrin-de-Puycousin* saved this tradition from being lost. His collections have been divided up between Dijon – where they are the heart of the excellent «Museum of Burgundian Life» – and his home town of Tournus. The pottery and copper is there to teach us a significant lesson, just like the wicker articles which are still sold in the town's shops today. The picture of daily life, when it is a beautiful one, can become the expression of an intelligent harmony. It was actually in the Tournus region, at *Villars*, that Anatole France set the final scene of the «Rotisserie de la Reine Pédauque», a monument of graceful scepticism. You should enter the *Greuze* and *Perrin-de-Puycousin* museums with the deeply-felt sense of respect which should be given to a people's roots.

(Above) Brancion: the covered market and the church in the castle. (Left) Chapaize: the geniality of a parish bell-tower.

THE ROMANESQUE VILLAGES

The region of Tournus, going up the Saône valley towards the hills, is a unique collection of landscapes which have been inhabited since ancient times. In each parish, the *church* is a masterpiece of Romanesque art. Often the *village* itself, perfectly preserved, is quite charming. Travel westwards and take time to discover this area. The debt this privileged land owes to *Cluny* will strike you immediately, but try to observe it with a more familiar eye: see its population of vinegrowers, breeders and hunters. «*Les gentilshommes chasseurs*», one of the short stories written by the Marquis of Foudras, makes essential reading. Whoever has not read the story of the «*Pauvre défunt Mr le curé de Chapaize*», will never know how happy life was before the industrial age... At **Brancion**, the church, castle, market and peasants' houses have perfectly preserved their medieval form; **Saint-Martin de Chapaize** and its XIth century bell-tower rise up out of the forest; **Lancharré** and its poignant «beguinage» of noble ladies, is abandoned; at **Ameugny**, the choir is signed, thus: «Seguin, creator of stones at Malay», in the XIIth century priorate and the modern Church of the Reconciliation at **Taizé**, the only Protestant monastic community in the world welcomes tens of thousands of young people every year.

Cormatin, the castle.

A wood painting inside the castle.

CORMATIN

Nobody loved Burgundy better than one of its sons: *Alphonse de Lamartine.* Everything in his life and works which irritates: a boat trip with the – almost – unfaithful wife of a member of the Institute, the homilies to God and the People, which the form does not always manage to save, the political illusions which involved him in a failed revolution, cannot make us forget his passionate loyalty to his homeland. The sorrowful song of *Milly,* the house next door: «*Faut-il le prononcer ce nom de la patrie...*» is a marvellous hymn to Burgundy and its arid hills, shady valleys, vines heavy with grapes and lime-trees forgotten by the ploughshares, on the slopes of a coombe. The shadow of the great poet can be felt at *Cormatin.* His house is very sumptuous. Built at the beginning of the XVIIth century, in a moderately Renaissance style, the valuable furniture and beautiful interiors have been preserved. It belonged to a romantic cloak and dagger character, the *Baron of Cormatin,* who fought with Washington and the Chevalier of Charette in two wars: the American War of Independence and the war of the Catholic and Royal Army of Vandée, which are not often associated... His descendant, *Ninon di Pierreclau,* was the great love of Lamartine. The excellent Burgundian writer, Roger Gouze, tells of his touching destiny in the delicate *Impromptu de Cormatin,* which is performed each summer.

Berzé-le-Châtel.

LEGENDARY MACONNAIS

The Saône at *Mâcon* is quite imposing. In July, its basin hosts international boat-races. The town has a certain charm and is an excellent starting point for discovering this legendary region. Do not be deceived by all the water: you are in the middle of a great vineyard. Who has not heard of the two small communes of *Pouilly* and *Fuissé*, firmly settled on their rock? The Mâconnais area produces some great wines. It ends, according to historical and administrative Burgundy, with *Romanèche-Thorins* (15 kilometres to the south) which shares, with its neighbour, Chenas, in the Rhône area, the first of the nine «grands crus» of *Beaujolais*: the *Moulin à Vent*. Beaujolais – an independent duchy – stretches down towards Lyon: it is even said that with the Saône and the Rhône it is the «third river» of the capital of the Gauls. But its vine-growers, who are particularly brilliant and gifted in «communications», work in close contact with their Burgundian cousins. Therefore, Mâcon can be considered a great wine-making centre with its *National French Wine Fair* in May, the *Wine Festival* on the first Sunday of September, the permanent *Wine Houses*, and its large trade.

Follow the hill road to the west. One of the first villages you will reach is *La Roche-Vineuse*... Lamartine owned some vineyards here, around *Milly* and the castle of *Saint-Point*. His vineyards were so important to him that in September 1848 – when he was a minister and candidate for President of the Republic... – he turned his attention towards his land. Since the grapes were ripe, he wrote to his nieces: «Take care of the harvesting of my three vineyards and proceed with the pressing. Give the vine-dressers in advance what they need to procure their bread for this winter. Place a total of one thousand eight hundred, two thousand bottles of wine in my cellars... Tell my vine-dressers that in my heart I am with them and this beautiful harvest, and that an abundance of everything will make the winter less hard for the poor.»

The two «Berzé» look down onto the valley. At **Berzé-la-Ville**, the «Monk's Chapel», an ancient Cluniac

Views of Mâcon, on the banks of the Saône.

priorate, offers an impressive sight: its XIIth century *frescoes*. Unfortunately, many of the colours have disappeared from the medieval monuments. «We know» that the church vault was painted with stars, the walls decorated with visions, the prophets dressed in scarlet. But we cannot «see them». Outside of Italy, what remains of the violently coloured abbatial monuments? Here, the «*Christ en majesté*» stands out amidst the Apostles in the centre of the constellations. Leaning towards the choir are the deacons, Vincent and Laurence, some bishops and pious women whose costumes strangely recall those of the Empress Theodora in the Byzantine mosaics at Ravenna. This refined art derives from many origins: portraits of Coptic Egypt, holy processions of Constantinople, the Carlovingian tradition of Reichenau and Trier, sublimed with a new certainty: an admirable symbol of XIIth century Christian faith! «Men of war» fought at *Berzé-le Châtel. Georges Duby* showed that at times the Devil marched in their ranks.

The rock of Solutré and Pouilly-Fuissé.

SOLUTRE

The high *rock of Solutré* dominates the landscape. Do not forget that all the surrounding vineyards are Pouilly-Fuissé! I am sure that you will easily find the courage to make the ascent...

This is one of the most ancient sites in the world. Students of prehistory gave the name «Solutrean» to the culture which developped in Stone Age Europe – between 20.000 and 15.000 years before our time. Its identification mark is a perfectly worked oval point, which has been defined as a «laurel leaf». Our Solutrean ancestors were great hunters, and the cunning needed in order to hunt game led them to gather together in an organized community. Of course, Solutré was only one of their settlements, but it is one of the most fascinating ones. Their prey was the *wild horse*, which emigrated in huge herds when the mountains of the east began to freeze in the winter. Man waited for the hordes to come up the west bank of the Saône. The seemingly insane stallions hurled themselves against the reindeer horns with silica handles. On the great stone slabs especially prepared for the slaughter, the fires burned all night... The great hunt lasted for millenniums. Around the «Crôt du Charnier», the bones of hundreds of thousands of these hairy ponies, which are depicted on the grotto walls, are amassed over several metres of land...

More complex civilizations developped along the banks of the river. They found safety and proximity to fishing areas by building their *lake-villages*, on palafittes, on the lagoons of the river. More structured communities settled on the heights behind the *walls* of dried stones. They had war lords, priests, paupers: the modern world was born... In the Vth century this world was shaken by the invasions of the barbarians. The *Burgondes*, those «Princes of the Clouds» who gave Burgundy its name, rest here in the big cemetery of *Charnay-les-Mâcon*. Gigantic warriors brandishing their iron swords; stocky Asians – the *Huns* – their companions and servants; and, to one side, a young man and woman, who entered Eternity with a hand resting on the shoulder of their companion...

Archaeology is the liveliest historical science. At Solutré, a *site museum* evokes these important moments of the human adventure. The landscape should be interpreted from a *high viewpoint*: the fields entrenched by obscure centuries, the Roman villages, the ever fertile vineyards. Towards the west there is the *Brionnais*. This small district of Burgundy gave life to some bright figures: starting with *Semur-en-Brionnais* and *Anzy-le-Duc*. It had a grandiose posterity. The abbot Renaud, son of the lord of Semur, was entrusted with the building of a great church, to become the destination for pilgrimages in northern Burgundy. A Cluniac, he would have done better to privilege the spiritual elevation of his Order. Instead he chose the luminous harmonies of the land of his childhood. And so the masterpiece of western Christian art was born: the *Basilica of Magdalen of Vézelay*.

(Above) The town of Cluny; (right) the Holy Water
Bell-Tower in the ancient abbey.

CLUNY

Here stood God's biggest dwelling on earth.

At the beginning of the Xth century, the Duke William the Pious donated his hunting pavilion to the «apostles Peter and Paul», «on condition that a regular monastery be built in that place in their honour, and that monks living according to the rule of Saint Benedict should gather there». Two centuries later, Cluny reigned over the Christian world. The «second Rome» controlled one thousand five hundred monasteries in the West. When consecrating the main altar of the basilica, in 1095, Pope Urban II was able to apply the following words from the Scriptures to his Cluniac brothers: «*You are the light of the world*». The great abbots – a race of saints – expressed God's will. From *Odon* to *Peter the Venerable*, they never stopped creating a wonderful building of stone, science and prayer.

At the height of its glory, in the XIIth century, the great abbatial church, the mother house of the Order, with its seven towers, two transepts and five naves, was the biggest in all Christendom, second only, by a small margin, to Bramante and Michelangelo's church of *Saint Peter*. The superiority granted to a combative liturgy gave the offices an imperious splendour. Perfection of the forms, the rites, the assured voices, but above all,

a violent expression of faith. The monks, who gathered together eight times by day and by night, did not sing with tremulous voices a «Gregorian chant» made insipid by the suspected sweetness of romanticism, they did not mumble syrupy songs, nor did they dream about approximative translations of the war songs of Israel: *they fought, untiringly, against the Devil*. When the «Lord of the Flies» managed to convince everyone that the Devil did not exist, Cluny lost all of its significance.

And so it was pulled down. The *Holy Water Bell-tower* which now seems so huge, was just one side tower in the midst of others, and not even the highest one... The Revolution drove out the monks. Later, others destroyed their house of prayer. Why? «There is no point in looking for a noble motive for an action when you have already found a base one», wrote Edouard Gibbon, who lived more or less around the time of this tragedy. The sculptured capitals depicting the lessons of Sibyl, the architraves with David dancing in front of the Arc, the tympanums illuminating the Prophets with their faces turned – after such a long wait – towards the Messiah, made excellent stones for gravelling the roads.

You must, however, visit *Cluny*, a marvel struck by

lightning, «ambulatory of the angels», ruined city of God, where only prayer remains.

The comparison between the abbot of Clairvaux, *Saint Bernard* and the abbot of Cluny, *Peter the Venerable*, is of great importance in the spiritual history of the XIIth century. They knew each other, they esteemed each other, they both believed in one God. They corresponded a lot: the «white monk» wrote with effusion and anguish, the «black monk» with slight restraint and some irony. The Cistercian was animated by a violent faith: «*Let your word be yes or no. All the rest comes from the Devil*». The Cluniac knew that the Devil's cunning is boundless and that certainty is a part of it... He welcomed *Abélard* to Cluny, that brilliant and rash theologian who had experienced human love with *Héloïse* and believed he could measure Divine love using Christian philosophy as a guide. Saint Bernard had «ex-

(Opposite page): (above) the abbatial palace (XVth century) now the site of the Ochier Museum and the Centre of Roman Studies; (below) the convent buildings (XVIIth century).

The Granary (XIIIth century) with the model of the abbey; (below) the Lapidarium.

(Left) The Bourbons' Chapel, built in the XVth century; (above) a detail of one of the corbels which originally made up the base of the statue. (Below) another interesting building inside Cluny abbey.

(Right) The Holy Water Bell-Tower.

ecuted» him, literally: at the Council of Sens the master fainted under his imprecations; at Paris, his best pupils abandoned him for Clairvaux. This is what was discussed at Cluny when God lived there.

What is done there today is not of small importance. Peter the Venerable would have appreciated the «*école d'ingénieurs*», just as he appreciated spiritual things. Saint Bernard would not have remained impassive before the stallions of the *National Equine Stud-farm* which protects the draught – and saddle – horse breeds of Burgundy. One day, while he was preaching in a Catharist village of Languedoc, the «Perfect ones» reproached him for the powerful neck of his horse. The son of the lord of the castle of Fontaine was a poor man among paupers, but he still certainly did not ride a broken-down horse...

(Left) The church of Notre-Dame; (below) the old streets of the town centre.

(Above right) The "Tour Ronde" and the "Tour Fabry" (1347); (below) "Haras national", national equine stud-farm.

Façade of the church.

BROU

The department of Ain, at the gates to Savoy and Switzerland, only became a part of Burgundy in the final period of the «Ancien Régime». However, its most prestigious monument, the *church of Brou* (at Bourg-en-Bresse), belongs to Burgundy, at its most ambitious, in its conception as well as its realization. It was the last dream of the Great Dukes of the West, the testimony of the fusion of the genius of the north with the splendour of the south, a Carthusian monastery of Champmol delivered from the barbarians. This shrine in perforated stone was built by *Margaret of Austria* in honour of her love for *Philibert of Savoy*.

In January 1477, Duke *Charles the Bold* was killed under the walls of Nancy. The French armies marched towards the north east. Arras and Dole burnt. Riots broke out in the towns of the Low Countries and the concillors of the great kingdom were beheaded in Gand Square. A young woman of twenty, *Mary*, inherited Burgundy. Loyal to her father's wishes, she married *Maximilian of Habsburg*, the Emperor's son. Together, with the support of the town armies and popular sentiment, they saved nearly everything, except for the old duchy around Dijon, from the ambitions of Louis

XI. Mary's reign lasted the length of a smile. Long enough, however, for her to entrust the destiny of the «kingdom of the Golden Fleece» to two children: Philip and Margaret. Philip the Handsome, Duke of Burgundy and Count of Flanders, married the heiress of the *Catholic Kings* and became the father of *Charles V.* Margaret had a happy life, with some sad parts, revealing herself to be an extraordinary woman.

Brought up in Amboise to be Queen of France, she was taken to Burgos to become Queen of Spain. One day, at last, she had a real husband, the Duke of Savoy, *Philibert the Handsome*. He was strong, enthusiastic and passionate. And also rather naïve... His State – Turin, Geneva, Chambery – occupied a strategic position in Europe. The Sforzas, the Medicis, the popes, the councils of Berne and Basle and the kings, surrounded him with conspiracies. They even enlisted the nearest in line to the throne, the dangerous *Bastard of Savoy*. Soon Margaret took charge of unearthing plots, unveiling traitors, and arranging surveillance of the castles. She was only twenty years old and already had such determination in the art of ruling... Life for her was a beautiful feast at the side of a handsome, generous and

Views of the two cloisters (XIVth and XVIth century).

loving man.

He died. Thus, for nearly twenty-five years Margaret reigned alone over the Low Countries, in the name of her Dynasty. The immense empire born of the encounter between the Valois of Burgundy, the Habsburgs and the Catholic Kings, was so vast that «the sun never set» on it. It was also an impossible empire, at the same time the homeland of Torquemada and Luther, Cortez and Montezuma... For around a quarter of a century, its lords were Margaret's father, brother and nephew. She guaranteed order for them in the rich and pacific Burgundian heart of their turbulent dominions. *Erasmus* was at home at the capital town of *Malines*, and when he was entrusted with the education of *Charles of Gand*, she chose a tutor for him, *Adrian of Utrecht*. In order to evaluate her influence, just remember that the tutor became Pope *Adrian VI*, and the pupil, Emperor *Charles V*. In 1529, she gave Europe the «Ladies' Peace». Yet, in secret, she wrote some beautiful verses, in the clear French of the Val de Loire of her childhood:

> «*Le temps est long et scay bien le pourquoi
> Où est mon coeur qui n'est plus avec moi.*»

(Above) Stained glass windows depicting Philibert the Handsome and Margaret of Austria. (Left) The tomb of Margaret of Bourbon.

The imperious Regent, who marked the great deeds of history with her tragic seal: «*Fortune, Infortune, Fort Une*», fostered an impassioned project: to dedicate a monument to her love, in the Burgundian tradition, with a magnificence made poignant by its expression of a true passion.

Margaret of Austria conceived *Brou* very soon after the death of Duke Philibert in 1504. She repeated exactly the same procedure followed by her ancestor, *Philip the Hardy* at Champmol, over a century earlier. She turned to the best masters of Bresse, the King of France's architect, *Jean Perréal*, the sculptor of the tombs of the Dukes of Brittany, *Michel Colombe*, the «clever and expert master mason», *Loys van Boghem* and other craftsmen of Brussels: *Jan van Room, Conrad Meyt*, and the Tuscans, *Tommaso and Mario Mariotto*. The stained glass windows were entrusted to *Nicolas Rambouts* who created the windows for Sainte-Gudule of Brussels, and a workshop in Lyon whose works are to be found in many churches from that of Saint-Nicolas-de-Port in Lorraine to the Cathedral of Aosta... Burgundian Europe – still very much alive – was not a juxtaposition of sly and chauvinist national cultures: the powerful breeze of creation still circulated freely around it.

The «plan» is a unique one. Only a woman could have

created it. In the axis of the choir, under the high vault, rests the *Duke of Savoy*, dressed as a Prince with an ermine cloak and the necklace of the Virgin Mary. His head is turned towards the tomb in which Margaret was laid to rest. On the level below, there is a nude and almost concealed corpse in a flamboyant style of architecture, signifying that the death of such a beautiful body is, always, unacceptable. To the right, there is *Margaret of Bourbon*, the mother of Philibert the Handsome, resting on a slab of marble, supported by weeping figures, with a greyhound at her feet. There is a lot of serenity and some indifference... To the left, a canopy of stupendous virtuosity hosts the tomb of *Margaret of Austria*. The higher statue depicts the Regent, who is proud of having served her Dynasty and who accepts no judgement other than that of God; the image on the ground next to her is that of a young woman, similar to many others for whom life has meant sorrow and separation: the Princess with the blood of the Dukes of Burgundy and the Germanic-Roman Emperors looks up to heaven; *Margaret's eyes gaze at Philibert's tomb.* More than the history, full of noise and fury, of the conqueror sovereigns, let us preserve the image of these two figures lying and looking at each other; these princes, our brothers and, like us, the sons of memory and oblivion, who desperately loved one another.

(Right) The tomb of Margaret of Austria. (Below) The last gothic episodes before the Renaissance.

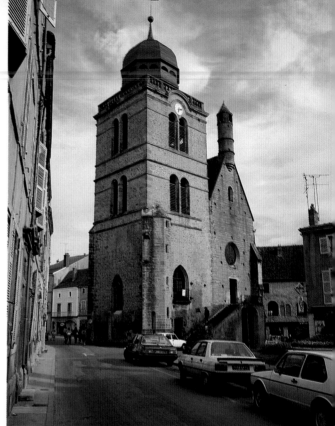

The Jaillet Palace (XVIth century).

The Tour Saint-Nicolas (XVIth century).

(Right) The Basilica of the Sacred Heart (Notre-Dame).

PARAY-LE-MONIAL

The great abbatial church of Cluny has been pulled down. But the school of architects and artists who were inspired by it have multiplied their lessons: from village churches to collegiate town churches: Notre-Dame of Beaune or Saint-Lazare d'Autun. But nowhere is the influence of Cluny as strong as at Paray-le-Monial.

The *church*, initially dedicated to the Virgin Mary, was built according to the will of *Saint Hugh*, the most ambitious constructor of the Cluniac XIIth century. It is still intact today, and can be seen as a «model» of Cluny. From the banks of the Bourbince, the austere façade with its two towers and powerful bell-tower boldly dominate. At sunset, in particular, the golden stone vibrates in the light. The calm waters offer a reflexion of Paray. You can easily carry out the following exercise of imagination: «rebuild» *two* or *three Parays* – seven towers, a nave with five parallels, 177 metres long (Saint Peter's in Rome is 186 metres long), three hundred windows – and, for a fleeting moment, *Cluny* will come to life again, just for you. But Paray is a lot more than a memory. Abbot Hugh's church has its own personality which is evident in the high triple elevated nave, of extraordinary conception. For architects and medievalists, it is a book of technical exploits which they never tire of reading. In effect, this balance is the result of a refined science of construction. Let us simply measure its admirable silence.

Christian faith – another legacy of Cluny, the Church of Saints and not of stones – has never stopped fervently believing in Paray-le-Monial. At the end of the XVIIth century, a young nun from the Convent of the Visitation, *Marguerite-Marie Alacoque*, had a vision of Christ. A strong and scandalous image struck her: «*This heart which so loved men*». God does not consult experts of communication and is not «skilful» in a human sense. The devotion to the *Sacred Heart* was unlucky... At that time the best Christians studied at the school of Jansenism, which gave an austere and elitist training; the worst believed that the time had come to enjoy oneself. The revelations of the nun at Paray were incongruous. The Church itself took a long time to recognize them: only *Joan of Arc* caused as much suspicion in Rome as mother *Marguerite-Marie*... The simple people were the ones to take a stand: the population of Marseilles since 1722, the heroic peasants of the Vandée wars in 1793, the signatories of the «National Vote» built, after 1870, the Basilica of the Sacred Heart at Montmartre. The intellectuals, especially the religious ones, have never liked God talking directly to his people. The emblem of the *Sacred Heart* took on a «right wing» connotation in the social and political fantasies of the French. But sarcasm was not enough to discourage the fervent crowds who gathered at Paray, singing:

«Sauvez Rome et la France
Au nom de Sacré-Coeur...».

The charismatic renewal has swept away these hostile attitudes. In October 1986, Pope *John Paul II*, before a huge crowd of pilgrims, greeted the *Community of Emmanuel* and received a resounding ovation. In the month of July, especially, old Paray is animated by mass demonstrations and the *Christian Festival of Art*. Saint Abbot Hugh would be pleased...

ANZY-LE-DUC

At Paray-le-Monial, the *Hiéron* museum contains an interesting collection of Christian art. The tympanum of the Church of *Anzy-le-Duc* found refuge there after the Revolution.

You need to travel southwards – for around twenty kilometres – in order to discover a Burgundy of pasture-land and springs, which is very different from the well-known image of vineyards and castles. Early on a Thursday morning, you should go to *Saint-Christophe-en-Brionnais*. This is where the biggest market of white Charolais cattle is held. Elsewhere computers fix the prices, and cheques transfer the ownership of poor beasts crammed with anabolic steroids; financiers who have never seen a real hedge or a meadow, play a Brussels «return» against a subsidy for Soviet consumers: you can contemplate the disaster in your tax return and in your plate. Here, breeders and dealers who can calculate the weight and quality of an animal at a *glance*, conclude their business in *silence*. Soon after, at the «café», bank-notes pulled out of wallets with worn edges are exchanged... The tradition of excellence, for the moment, still holds good.

The church of Anzy-le-Duc: the portal and the octagonal bell-tower.

The mallet of Creusot.

The **Church of Anzy-le-Duc** was built between the XIth and XIIth centuries. All of Brionnais' creativity – it is the source of Vézelay – is revealed here in its loyalty to its Cluniac origins. The octagonal bell-tower is a marvel. Stop off at **Montceaux-l'Etoile** whose tympanum depicts the Ascension. Two angels point up to heaven... The national school of civil aviation at *Saint-Yan* could have used them as its emblem. The school trains pilots for French and African airline companies: Burgundy is not only the past!

LE CREUSOT

Towards the north, you will come to a highly industrialized region. Beginning with the coal of *Montceau* in the XVIIIth century, this has been one of the poles of French development. The annexation of Alsatia and Lorraine to the German Empire in 1871 made Burgundy, which was better protected, the centre of the arms industry. Locomotives continued to be built there, but so were the cannons of the *Reconquest*. A booklet entitled «*Tour de France de deux enfants*», formed the people of the «Great War». The «black hussars» of the Republic, some tens of thousands of fanatical teachers, used the passage which tells of *Julien* and *André's* sensations when they see the great **mallet** of Le Creusot, for dictation: «Oh! Mr Gestal, I see that Burgundy works well and I think that if France is a great nation, it is because all the provinces do their best to...» Today Le Creusot manufactures wagons for high speed trains: 320 kilometres an hour from Paris to London and Brussels, from Madrid to Seville, from Marseilles to Strasbourg...

The **Ecomuseum of Glassware** tells it all, from the crystalware of Louis XVI to the Schneider empire, which had schools, bands, loan funds and even their own statues in the squares. Plus strikes and clashes: *this is the temple of the memory of the workers.*

(Left) Two views of Autun. (Above) The church of Saint-Lazare, the most beautiful collection of images in the Western Romanesque style.

AUTUN

Autun is really the true capital of Burgundy, due to its antiquity and authenticity.

At the time of Celtic independence, the *Aedui* declared themselves to be the «allies of the Senate and the Roman People». They despised the *Lingons* of the north, the inhabitants of the huts on which Dijon would one day stand. They feared the *Sequani*, on the other side of the Saône, already a turbulent people like their descendants, the Comtois. They entertained relationships of power with the *Bituriges* – the «kings of the world» – to the west and with the troublesome *Arverni*. They were attracted by Rome. The «*Provincia*» was not so far away, with its triumphal columns, trading basilicas where products from the Orient were amassed, and *villae* surrounded by vineyards where aristocrats, dressed in white togas on which the purple band of the senatorial order stood out, walked amidst slaves bent over the vines...

They looked at the world from their fortress at *Bibracte*, above the beech-woods. The horizon of the walls stretched from the origins of the *Seine* in the north to the already capricious course of the *Loire* in the south. Opposite the rising sun they could see the Saône plain, the Jura mountains and, beyond, the dangerously fertile East... For millenniums, civilizations rose out of the eastern steppe, with their gods, forms and new dreams. The heart of Asia launched its Messianic

hordes towards Europe, bringing techniques which told of the existence of another way of thinking: the point of an arrow, a procedure for melting bronze, a winged horse on a queen's tiara. In 59 B.C. a new threat emerged: the *Helvetians* had set fire to their twelve citadels and their four hundred villages and had taken the road to the west. The Aedui chose Rome.

At the foot of the abandoned fortress of Bibracte they founded their new capital *Augustodunum*, Autun. The actual name of the town: the ancient Gallic word for «fortress», together with the Emperor's patronymic, its motto «*soror et aemula Romae*» and its layout, show their desire to emulate their conquerors. It became one of the most important towns in the west with its *forum*, Capitolian temple, palaces, houses decorated with marble and mosaics, two theatres, circus, and the imposing walls over six kilometres long interrupted by monumental gates. Schools of great renown established themselves here. One of their teachers, *Eumene*, was a minister of the Emperor Constance in the IIIrd century. His shrewd fellow-countrymen asked him to intervene in order to protect, from the revenue authorities, the great properties of the *clarissimae* which stretched, with regard to the vineyards, as far as the Côte of the «*pagus arebrignus*»: Beaune and Nuits Saint-Georges. He managed to do this by beginning his speech with that figure of Roman rhetoric destined to have great success: the

The church of Saint-Lazare: the tympanum and capitals.

(Right) The Rolin Museum: (below) Eve lying down, by the mysterious "Gislebertus".

«*captatio benevolentiae*» which the Americans use as an *opening joke: «they think we're rich...»*

Autun naturally became the seat of the *bishopric of Burgundy.* In 1789, its owner was still the «born-prince» of the «Etats» representing the Province. He was a very singular person: *Maurice de Talleyrand-Périgord,* who had a prestigious career throughout the storms of the Revolution, the Empire and the monarchies of the XIXth century: his mind was certainly worth more than his soul. His predecessors, who believed in God, had built the **Cathedral of Saint-Lazare**, a masterpiece of Romanesque art. We can understand just how baffling this vision, rooted in the land of the Celts, nourished by an ancient culture and reinvented by Cluny, can be by reading these notes made by *Stendhal* in front of the capitals of Autun: «God! How ugly...»

Saint-Etienne was begun around 1120 by the bishop, Etienne de Bagé, who had been fascinated by the building yard at Cluny. *Pope Innocent II* consecrated the first altar in the midst of stone-cutters and carts. Despite the many readjustments and additions – up until the XVIth century – the building still preserved its Romanesque mark. The motif on the *Arroux Gate* was copied for the arch of the triforium and for an external mural decoration; everywhere old style fluted pillars have replaced encased columns. The *sculptures,* a sort of stone Bible, this side of Rome, are out of the dark ages. A tremendous personality – attested by a vague signature: *Gislebertus* – gave them a dramatic dimension. The *capitals* should be read one by one, taking time to grasp the symbolic inspiration in the subtle references, with the *Autun* of Canon Grivot. There is no need for an intermediary to appreciate the freedom and simplicity – signs of genius – of the renowned *Universal Judgement* on the tympanum and the architrave of the western portal.

The **Rolin Museum** is exciting. It should count amongst its treasures of Autun's illustrious past, the *Virgin of Chancellor Rolin* by Jan van Eyck, the unforgettable confrontation of the minister of the Dukes of Burgundy, in a brown and gold brocade suit, and the nude Child on his mother's knee. Napoleon decided that this painting, which the compassionate *Rolin* family of Autun had destined for the cathedral, «was too beautiful to stay in the provinces» and had it assigned to the Louvre. However, just the *Eve lying down*, on one of Saint-Lazare's architraves, is enough to motivate a visit. This is the most feminine sculpture of the Romanesque Middle Ages, the most seductive and perfect medieval nude, the *Olympia* of the XIIth century. The Primitive Hall contains the *Nativity* by the Master of Moulins and the *Virgin of Autun* which is still discreetly marked by its XVth century polychromy. The very interesting collection of XIXth century paintings is being constantly enriched. The Museum itself, located in the palace belonging to the famous family which gave Beaune its Hôtel-Dieu, is quite charming. And with its three masterpieces: *Eve lying down*, the *Nativity* and the *Virgin*, it is also quite unforgettable. Do not forget to visit Roman, medieval, classical Autun – with the surprising XIXth century touch of its renewed *shopping arcade* – a dignified and lively town, which has been very well preserved. You will see children wearing sky-blue service caps: they are pupils of the *military college* located in the ancient castle. They are preparing, through important scientific studies, to become officials of the armies of the Republic. They are allowed to dream: Bonaparte was one of them...

The Rolin Museum: Our Lady, the Nativity by the Master of Moulins and Saint Catherine.

(Right) Roman Autun: the theatre and the Arroux Gate.

The castle of Sully.

(Right) two views of Châteauneuf.

THE CASTLES OF BURGUNDY

Along the roads, which now begin to diverge, you will find road signs with «Castles of Burgundy» written in white letters on a brown background, followed by the name of the monument. You will discover some splendid sites: *fortresses* of the Dark Ages in which illustrious families had their great fiefs and lands, the *fortified houses* of soldiers of fortune who loved tournaments and brigandage, luminous open *galleries* built by warriors on their return from Acre or Naples in memory of an Eastern love, classical *palaces* for the «Treasures of France» or the presidents of Parliament, *follies* for the infidelities of Louis XV's chevaliers and gallant abbots, neo-Gothic *manor-houses* built by readers of «Génie du Christianisme» and «milliard des Emigrés»... Three examples, randomly chosen along the route...

Sully – on the road between Autun and Beaune – was built at the beginning of the XVIth century by the noble *Saulx-Tavannes* family. «It is, wrote Madame de Sévigné, the Fontainebleau of Burgundy». The grounds, water and façades create a quiet harmony. The *Marshal of Mac-Mahon* was born here and the present owners are his descendants. Italy is in his debt for the help he gave, at *Magenta* and *Solferino*, in the «Risorgimento»; France, of which he was the second – monarchic – president of the IIIrd Republic, is also in his debt for having

tried, not without being ridiculed, to reconcile his country.

Châteauneuf-en-Auxois – on the old road between Autun and Dijon – is the «castle in the village» of the medieval miniatures from the flamboyant century of the Dukes. It was the scene for the dark story of a lonely young lady of the castle who betrayed her dreadful husband. The «*Roman de la Dame de Vergy*» rendered this situation familiar to the people of Burgundy. In the evenings, jesters described the amusing intrigue of the griffin which was raised in order to warn the lover of the bothersome husband's absence and sang the following lines in the rhythm of a «ring-dance»:

> «*Les venus a les allées*
> *et la convenance première*
> *et du petit chien la manière...*»

These stories do not usually have a happy ending. The «dame de Vergy» died «*for having faithfully loved her friend*»; the lady of the castle of Châteauneuf was beheaded. The Duke was probably not displeased to retake possession of this strong point. In the village, you should stop off at the *inn* – a peaceful place whose cuisine and cellars deserve your attention – and at the smiling and

The castle of Commarin.

(Above right) The basilica of Saint-Andoche and the Romanesque capitals. (Below) the Bull by Pompon.

competent *antiquarian's* shop.

Commarin on the same road – is the birth-place of *Henry Vincenot*, author of «Billebaude» and «Pape des escargots». He really took it all to heart! The *castle*, built on a very ancient site, goes back essentially to the XVIIth century. It is a beautiful private residence and the Count and Countess of Vogüé have managed to preserve its charm. Marie-Judith de Vienne, Marquise of Antigny, who lived here in the XIIIth century, did not notice the passing of time. The *Viennes* fought for the Great Dukes of the West with this magnificent war cry: «*Saint Georges au puissant duc!*». Go and see the *wolf* killed in the castle grounds in 1916: the past is not so old...

SAULIEU

You are now on the road which heads northwards, across pasture-land bordered by hedges where, for three years, the *white Charolais* cattle are nourished by the lymph of the land and the dew of the skies. This breed of bovines, created for gastronomists, produces an incomparable meat which is tasty and perfectly streaked with fat. Being used to «reform cows», the innocent victims of EEC «quotas» on milk production, and South American meat softened in the freezer, you should get ready for a surprise: maybe eating is not such hard work...

Saulieu has dedicated a statue to the Charolais. It chose – to be on the safe side and guarantee the breed... – the *Bull* by François Pompon (1855-1933), a superb work by this great animal sculptor whose artistic production is nearly all preserved in the Museum of Dijon. At the unveiling ceremony, in 1948, Edouard Herriot – who came out of a great school and was Mayor of Lyon, Prime Minister, and many other things... – made a wonderful speech. For those who know how to «decipher», its text was immortal: is should be included on the syllabus of all courses in French history and civilization. The **Hôtel de la Côte-d'Or** is rather like a temple. *Alexandre Dumaine* made it France's first table. *Bernard Loiseau* fights on the front line. As regards inventiveness he is, without doubt, already the winner. It is a pleasure for him not to be the only one fighting for a good cause: the hours spent in a Saulieu restaurant are not lost. Do not forget to visit **Saint-Andoche**. The XIIth century basilica was very badly treated by Edward IIIrd's English.

AVALLON

This is one of the «gates» of Burgundy, marvellously situated on a rocky spur dominating the *Cousin valley* which, with its castles and windmills, is a truly privileged place. In the town and the valley you can find the right foundations – from the very refined to the very spontaneous – for discovering the regions of Avallon and Morvan.

Saint Lazare is venerated here. A famous relic, brought to the town by Duke Henry of Burgundy, created such a great movement of pilgrims that it was necessary to build a large church. This was built in the XIIth century, naturally following the Cluniac model. The particularly imaginative decorations have been plundered. However, on the *main door*, angels and old musicians, signs of the Zodiac, and monthly labours, acanthus leaves and vine leaves still create a touching image.

It is necessary to take a walk around the **Ramparts** in order to understand what these medieval communities – who amassed so many illuminated stones – were really like. They lived in constant fear of war. Even though Duke Philip was the lord, in the heart of the XVth century, of seventeen dominions from Zuidersee to Jura, a «lost soldier» was enough to endanger his good towns. One of these soldiers, one of the cruellest, was Jacques d'Espailly, known as «*Fortespice*», who conquered Avallon by the «stairs». The *Virgin of Lacy* is worth seeing at the **Museum**: she marks the transition from the XIIIth to the XIVth century, the passage from smiling expressions to seriousness and melancholy.

VEZELAY

The *basilica of Magdalen*, consecrated eleven centuries ago, is situated on a hilltop. Set amidst the valleys, it looks like the Temple mentioned in the Bible: a holy house built close to heaven. «*I shall go up to the altar of God, the Lord, who is the joy of my youth...*» say the Scriptures, which also add: «*A man went up towards Jerusalem...*»

Charlemagne's heirs tore each other to pieces in the middle of the IXth century. Not far from here, at *Fontenay-en-Puisaye*, a fratricidal battle was not able to resolve the dispute. Through the *Oath of Strasbourg* – «*Pro deo amor...*» – they divided up Europe for a thousand years. It was then that the Count of Burgundy, *Girard*, built a monastery at Vézelay. His castle of *Mont Lassois* at Vix was near Châtillon-sur-Seine. On the plains, a forgotten tomb hosted a sleeping princess in her parade coach, her head girded by the golden tiara of the Scythians, and surrounded by the black vases of Etruria, the ochre goblets of Hellas and the great bronze crater on which the horsemen of «Panathenaea» rode... *Girard de Rousillon* was himself a legendary hero. His «Gestures» were as famous as the *Chanson de Roland*. Pious institutions seemed more necessary than blows of a sword. It was thought that the world was growing old in a bad way:

The church of Saint-Lazare, the façade and the vestibule. (Below right) the Clock Tower.

The hill with the basilica of Sainte-Madeleine: the Spirit persists here.

On the following pages: the basilica of Sainte-Madeleine: the façade, the narthex, the nave and two capitals of the pillars (the mystical Mill and David riding a lion).

«Bons fut li sicles al tems ancïenour,
Quer fiez i eret e justice ed amours...»

In the middle of the XIth century, *Vézelay* received the relics of *Mary Magdalen*, the heavily made-up daughter of *Magdala*, on the banks of the *Kinereth*, who washed Christ's feet with rare perfumed essences, and to whom He said those words which still shock the bigots: *«Much will be forgiven her, for she has much loved...»* The Carlovingian church became too small and the monks – some dependant on Cluny, but most of them independants – built a huge church for the pilgrims, in the Brionnais style. The construction work lasted for the whole of the XIIth century. This church is the *marvel of the West*. In no other place has the Romanesque period managed to produce such harmony of creativity and technique. Observe for yourselves the sight of the nave, the light of the choir and the lesson of the capitals. Here, too much coherence in the explanations, too much insistence on commentaries, too much authority in the demonstrations would just serve to avert us from the

essentialities. Once, a cinematographer wanted to film the face of the *Christ en majesté* on the main tympanum. He worked for a long time in order to arrange very violent lighting. When at last he succeeded, all he actually obtained was the image of an almost expressionless stone: the sculptor had used the *shadow coming from the vault* as one of the materials of his creation.

When he heard that *Edessa* had fallen into the hands of the Muslims, the Pope ordered *Saint Bernard* to preach in favour of the Crusades. On 31st March 1146, from the clearing marked by a cross, the abbot of Clairvaux dragged a hundred princes and a hundred thousand paupers along the bitter roads to the East. *Philip Augustus* and *Richard the Lion Heart* concentrated their forces at Vézelay before leading them towards Jerusalem. *Philip the Good* and *Henry V of Lancaster* gathered their armies here too, but their objective was Paris:

«The world was good in the old times
When there was faith, justice and love...»

119

THE MORVAN REGIONAL PARK

French policy on *natural reserves* makes a distinction between *national parks* (7), which are kept in their natural state through the application of severe regulations, and *regional parks* (25) where human activity is allowed as long as it respects the environment. This means no pollutant industries but a rational exploitation of the forest; no spreading of toxic substances killing off the wild fauna, but a tolleration of hunting which, through selection, removes a small part of it; no poisoning of the rivers but a regulated and organized opening of the springs and lakes.

The *Morvan regional park*, in the heart of Burgundy, in the departments of Côte-d'Or, Yonne and Nièvre has, over the last twenty years, definetely managed to preserve the soul of the «land» whilst keeping its men in work. The «Maison du Parc» at *Saint-Brisson*, and its «gates» at *Avallon, Saulieu* and *Autun* propose itineraries for setting off on a voyage of discovery: timber transported by horses, walks on the *Black Mountain*, hides for watching the roe-bucks and wild boar, encounters at the *Abbey of Pierre-qui-Vire*, in a legendary land, with a community of anonymous monks who are altogether the world's foremost specialists in Romanesque art.

The mayor of *Château-Chinon*, François Mitterand, was elected President of the Republic of France in 1981 and 1988. This disproves the bad proverb of the inhabitants of Beaune which says «From Morvan comes neither good wind, nor good people».

(Above left) A lake in the Morvan Regional Park; (below) the Calvary of Château-Chinon.

Nevers, on the banks of the Loire.

NEVERS

Nivernais is a province. It heads in a westerly direction, bearing towards the course of the Atlantic Loire, thus deviating from Burgundy which, between the Seine and the Saône, has a north-south axis. The economic sluggishness, the originality of its «left-wing» orientated political temperament and some anger have done the rest.

But historical links are very strong. *Noviodunum* was an important Aedui market. The «dauphin» of the Dukes of Valois, *Monsieur Jean*, was Count of Nevers when, in 1392 at Nicopolis, during the desperate attack of the last Crusade against the Sultan's «volunteers of death», he won the title of «*Fearless*». A cadet branch of the House of Burgundy reigned over Nevers for many years: at its head, towards the end of the epos of the Great Dukes of the West, was an enigmatic prince-sorcerer who «evoked» demons which were strangely inclined to suggest that he should draw nearer to the King of France... The **ducal palace**, now the Law Courts, was finished in the XVIth century by the *Clèves* family whose legend was the story of the *Chevalier and the swan*:

> «*I see a glorious chevalier, enveloped in a splendid light*
> *His eyes look at me with kindness*
> *He stands amidst the clouds, leaning on a sword*
> *near a palace of gold...*»
> (Richard Wagner, *Lohengrin*, act I)

Marriage brought the third son of the Duke of Mantua, *Luigi di Gonzaga*, here. He introduced the art of ceramics through the *Corrado brothers of Savona* «master potters of works in white and other colours». The second half of the XVIIth century saw the triumph of *Nevers blue* (see the *museum* and collections all over the world). There have been many famous women: *Mary of Gonzaga*, twice Queen of Poland, and her goddaughter, *Marie de la Grange d'Arquian*, once Queen of Poland; *Bernadette Soubirous*, the touching visionary of *Lourdes* who, under the name of Sister Marie-Bernard, lived a reserved existence at the convent of Nevers where her body now rests; the same *Marguerite Duras* for whom Alain Resnais fixed the immobile horizons of «*Hiroshima mon amour*», on the banks of the Loire.

The **cemetery of Nevers** was famous. During the Terror of the Revolution, a Conventionalist on a mission decided to make it a symbol of the new times: the crosses would be knocked down and a single inscription would impart the sinister lesson that «*death is an eternal sleep*». Robespierre denounced this assault on hope. *Fouché* was recalled and, fearing that he could soon be

123

experiencing the sleep he boasted about at Nevers, he led the assault of *Thermidor* against the «Incorruptible». He had been a priest, he became a duke: he was basically just a policeman of no account.

The **cathedral of Saint-Cyr and Sainte-Julitte** recapitulates all the creative impulses of Christian monumental art between the Xth and XVIth centuries. Altogether the effect is rather strange but has a sublime grandeur. Some may prefer the solid Romanesque style of **Sainte-Etienne**. The old town is charming with its towers, doors, and «princes' ascent». The river flows towards the «Valley of the Kings», the magic land of castles along the Loire. Its course is still quite wild as adjustments have been made only further downstream. The *Duke of Edinburgh* declared that he was rather worried about these. His intentions were not badly received: at the time of the Hundred Years War, the town sided more with Burgundy and the English, than with the King of France...Many interesting discoveries can be made at Nevers. There is, obviously, river tourism along the Loire and the canals. Nearby are the castles of *Rozemont* (XIIIth century) and, more importantly, *Chevenon* (XIVth century): an austere sculpture with fascinating equilibriums. There is the fortified village of *Saint-Pierre-le-Moutier*, and the historic forges of *Guerigny*, the Navy's ship-yard which supplied the anchors for the King's ships up until those for the steamboat *France*. The French «Formula 1 Grand Prix» is held on the *Magny-Cours* circuit. To the west is the gentle slope of the *Morvan*, with its pools and castles, and *Decize* which saw the birth of the «Archangel of the Revolution», Saint-Just and the novelist who told of the suffering of those who fought in the trenches and the joy of the poachers, Maurice Genevoix («Les croix de bois», «Raboliot»).

(Above) The "Porte du Croux" (XIVth century) and one of the round towers of the Ducal Palace, (below) the apse of the church of Saint-Etienne (XIth century).

(Left) The cathedral of Saint-Cyr: the bell-tower and the apse.

The town walls of Chârité-sur-Loire.

THE CHARITE-SUR-LOIRE

If you have followed this itinerary of the heart and the history of Burgundy right from the beginning, then now is the time for us to part. There is some regret, on my part, because there are so many more things that I would have liked to have told you, and maybe some of these things would have touched you deeply. I shall never know what you liked, what you discovered, what the moment, the occasion showed you... On the old maps dating back to the times of the «Voyages towards new stars», when the white standard with the cross of Saint Andrew of the Dukes of Burgundy fluttered on the mast-head of ships, the world was almost entirely made up of coastlines: «dromes», bays and ports. The inland appeared as a huge white blob. A shape, a name, a legend were the only points of reference. For the whole of Africa, there were just these words: «*Hic sunt Elephantes.*» It is the best guide. It suggests the hot track with sharp grass still bent after the wild beast has passed, the lake from which, like a flight of gazelles, the evening's fire rises in the violent cry of the forest...

It could be, however, that your journey starts here.

You have just come from *Bourges* and are about to enter Burgundy. Let me tell you that there are many adventures in store for you. In 1429, the King of France, *Charles VII*, decided to seize *Charité-sur-Loire*, the *Duke of Burgundy's* first stronghold. The royal army was trained with a precision which was rare at that time in France. The town of Orléans, happy to be liberated, supplied a huge mortar and some archers. The naval battles were led by the best captains. *Joan of Arc*, on her white horse, oriflamme in her hand, commanded the attacks. Everything was ready for an historical victory which children would have piously recited in the schoolrooms of the Republic! Alas! They were miserably defeated. The winner was one of the Duke's squires, *Perrinet Gressart*, a commando leader whose life was a novel, just like that of his companions: François de Surienne, known as the Aragonese, Guiot Bernique, Jean de Saint-Sauflieu, known as Rabasche, Antoine de Roncheval, Jean d'Avril, Thomassin Duquesne and Pierre l'Espagnol... «Mgr de Bourgogne» kept *Charité-sur-Loire*, and after peace was made in 1435, the King still

The old stone bridge (XVIth century) and the "Tour Sainte-Croix" (XIIth century) at the entrance to the ancient abbey of La Charité. (Below) A view of the nave destroyed in 1559 and now occupied by dwellings.

wanted Perrinet Gressart to maintain his position as captain of the town. He addressed some courteous words to him which the «old man» listened to with his hand on the hilt of his sword: in those days, they did not catch the flies of Burgundy with vinegar... The basilica of Notre-Dame was damaged by fire (in the XVIth century) and by questionable restoration work; however what remains is of considerable interest. The «Charité des bons pères», with its work assisting the poor and pilgrims was in some ways Cluny's «first-born». Pope Pascal II consecrated the altar in 1107. The abbey was almost completely destroyed, or rather «absorbed» by the town from the XVIth century onwards; this is the reason for the unusual arches which one can run into at a bend in an alley. The old traditions remain, there are not yet any restaurants offering hamburgers, and the good eating places are still called *le Grand Monarque* (the Great Monarch), *le Bon Laboureur* (the Good Worker), *la Bonne Foi* (the Good Faith); hunt beatings «in pursuit, on the run and wearily» still liven the *forest of Bertranges*, with its secular oak-trees.

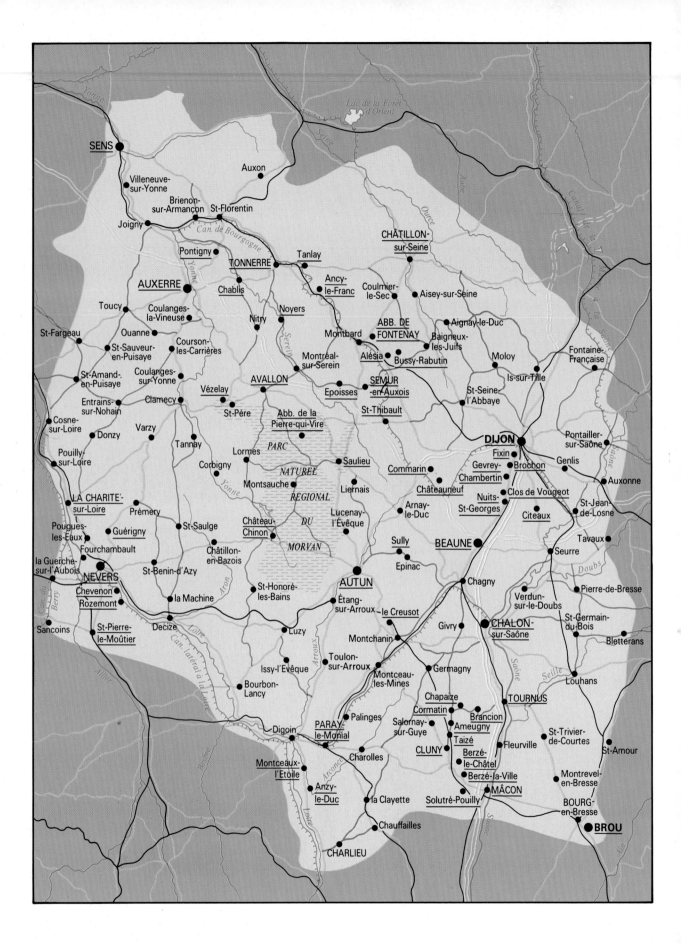